Microsoft Office
PowerPoint® 2007 Plain & Simple

Nancy Muir

PUBLISHED BY
Microsoft Press
A Division of Microsoft Corporation
One Microsoft Way
Redmond, Washington 98052-6399

Library of Congress Control Number: 2006937714

Printed and bound in the United States of America.

1 2 3 4 5 6 7 8 9   QWT   2 1 0 9 8 7

Distributed in Canada by H.B. Fenn and Company Ltd.

A CIP catalogue record for this book is available from the British Library.

Microsoft Press books are available through booksellers and distributors worldwide. For further information about international editions, contact your local Microsoft Corporation office or contact Microsoft Press International directly at fax (425) 936-7329. Visit our Web site at www.microsoft.com/mspress. Send comments to mspinput@microsoft.com.

Acquisitions Editor: Juliana Aldous Atkinson
Developmental Editor: Sandra Haynes
Project Editor: Kathleen Atkins
Project Manager: Joell Smith-Borne of Abshier House
Compositor: Ron Wise of Abshier House
Indexer: Sharon Hilgenberg of Abshier House

Body Part No. X12-65188

To my partner in life, Earl, for helping me survive writing five books in five months and even pitching in to get it all done. You are the best, sweetheart.

Contents

Acknowledgments xi

1 About This Book   1

No Techie Talk 1
A Quick Overview 2
A Few Assumptions 3
What's New in PowerPoint 2007? 3
The Final Word 4

2 What's New in PowerPoint 2007?   5

What's Where in PowerPoint 2007? 6
Using the Ribbon 8
Work with the Mini Toolbar 12
Customize the Quick Access Toolbar 14
Work with New Design Elements 17

3 Getting Started with PowerPoint 2007   23

Creating a New Presentation 24
Finding and Opening Existing Presentations 27
Sizing Panes in Normal View 29

What do you think of this book? We want to hear from you!

Microsoft is interested in hearing your feedback so we can continually improve our books and learning resources for you. To participate in a brief online survey, please visit:

www.microsoft.com/learning/booksurvey/

Viewing Multiple Slides with Slide Sorter. 31
Running a Presentation in Slide Show View 32
Saving and Closing a PowerPoint Presentation. 34
Getting Help. 36

4   Building a Presentation   37

Understand How to Build a Presentation. 38
Building a Slide. 38
Work with Text 42
Find and Replace Text 46
Manipulating Placeholders. 48

5   Building a Presentation Outline   53

Understanding the Relationship of the Outline to Slides 54
Working with the Outline. 54
Adding Text in the Outline Tab 56
Working with Outline Contents. 58

6   Managing and Viewing Slides   65

Viewing Slides in Slide Pane. 66
Managing Slides in Slide Sorter View 67
Hiding Slides and Slide Elements 70

7   Using Slide Layouts and Themes   73

What Slide Layouts and Themes Control 74
Work with Layouts. 76
Work with Themes 80
Change Theme Colors and Fonts 83

8 Inserting and Drawing Objects **87**

Creating Tables. 88
Edit Tables. 92
Creating Charts 96
Adding Clip Art 102
Creating WordArt 106
Working with SmartArt. 109
Working with Pictures. 112
Working with Media Objects 116
Create a Photo Album. 118
Drawing Shapes and Text Boxes 120

9 Formatting Text, Objects, and Slides **123**

Applying Fonts. 124
Formatting Text 126
Formatting Objects 130
Resizing Objects. 134
Rotate and Flip Objects. 135
Grouping and Changing the Order of Objects 136
Working with Picture Tools. 138
Changing the Slide Background 141

10 Working with Slide Masters **143**

Making Changes to a Slide Master 145
Adding and Deleting Master Sets 149
Working with Handout and Notes Masters. 152

11   **Adding Transition Animations**   **157**

     Applying a Transition 158
     Adding Sound to Transitions 160
     Modifying Transition Speed. 162
     Choosing How to Advance a Slide 163
     Apply a Custom Animation to an Object. 165
     Previewing an Animation 169

12   **Finalizing Your Slide Show**   **171**

     Reviewing Your Presentation 172
     Setting Up a Slide Show 178
     Rehearsing Your Presentation 182
     Taking a Presentation with You 185

13   **Running a Presentation**   **187**

     Starting and Ending a Slide Show. 188
     Navigating through Slides 191
     Working with the Pen and Annotations. 194
     Switching to Another Program 197

14   **Printing a Presentation**   **199**

     Inserting Headers and Footers. 200
     Using Print Preview 202
     Establishing Printer Settings and Printing 204

15   **Publishing a Presentation to the Web**   **209**

     Saving a Presentation as a Web Page. 210
     Publishing a Presentation as a Web Page 213

16   **Introducing Advanced PowerPoint Topics**   **215**

     Saving Your Own PowerPoint Templates 216
     Creating a Custom Show 217
     Removing Hidden Data with Document Inspector. 220
     Add a Digital Signature. 222

     Index 227

What do you think of this book? We want to hear from you!

Microsoft is interested in hearing your feedback so we can continually improve our books and learning resources for you. To participate in a brief online survey, please visit:

www.microsoft.com/learning/booksurvey/

Acknowledgments

Writing a book is always a team effort, but visual books like this one are especially so, with several folks reviewing and correcting text, laying out graphic elements, and making sure every callout goes to the right spot. Many thanks to Joell Smith-Borne for ably leading the team of editors, proofreaders, and graphic folks to keep us all on track. Thanks to Ron Wise for keeping the layout in line, Kelly Dobbs Henthorne for expert proofreading, and Chris Pichereau for ensuring that I got the technical facts straight. Finally, I want to thank Juliana Aldous for trusting me with the project, and Debbie Abshier for her leadership in producing several books in this series for Office 2007.

1

About This Book

In this section:

- No Techie Talk
- A Quick Overview
- A Few Assumptions
- What's New in PowerPoint 2007?
- The Final Word

If you are the typical PowerPoint user, you lead a hectic life, whether it's spent running from meeting to meeting and conference to conference, or from the soccer match to a volunteer committee meeting. If so, this book is for you. In *Microsoft PowerPoint Plain & Simple*, you get an easy-to-use reference that helps you get to work immediately. My goals are to help you get going with presentations right away and to provide you with information about all sorts of tools and features you can use to create even more sophisticated presentations over time.

This book is based on Microsoft Office PowerPoint 2007 installed on a Windows Vista operating system, but if you have earlier versions of Windows (preferably Windows XP with Service Pack 2 installed), you'll find most things work exactly the same. The exciting new interface that PowerPoint 2007 introduces makes your work easier to handle and offers some powerful visual tools for your presentations.

No Techie Talk

If you have a presentation deadline staring you in the face, the last thing you want is a lengthy lecture. You need to find out how to accomplish something quickly. This book is structured task by task to help you find what you need help with now and to keep you moving.

No task in this book will make you read more than two pages to find an answer to your question. Look up what you need to do in the table of contents or index, follow the steps in the task, and you're done. I don't spend lots of time on lengthy explanations, and you don't need a technical dictionary by your side to understand these steps.

Occasionally, you encounter a See Also element that refers you to a related task, simply because some functions overlap each other. There are also Tips here and there that provide advice. Finally, the Try This feature gives you ideas for how to put PowerPoint to use, and Cautions warn you of potential problems. But the main focus of this book is to keep you on track, providing the information you need quickly and simply.

Just Essential Tasks

The tasks in this book are organized logically for the types of things you do in PowerPoint. If you've never built a presentation, you could start at the beginning and work your way through to build your first slide show. But you don't have to move through the book in order. If you know exactly what you want to accomplish, just find that task and go to it!

...And the Easiest Way to Do Them

Although PowerPoint 2007 often gives you several ways to get things done, I've tried to suggest the easiest way to get results. The new PowerPoint 2007 interface has gotten rid of some methods, such as using menus and toolbars for most tasks, but keyboard shortcuts and contextual toolbars (tools that appear only when you are performing a certain type of task) are available to address different styles of working. Feel free to explore the interface and help system to find other ways of getting things done after you've mastered the basics!

A Quick Overview

Although you don't have to read this book from front to back (in fact, you probably won't), it's useful for you to understand how I've structured it so you can find your way around.

Once you have installed PowerPoint 2007 (an easy task because the Office installer guides you through step by step), you can begin exploring any of the following sections and their individual tasks.

Sections 2 and 3 introduce you to the PowerPoint interface (what you see on the screen) and how you move around and manipulate tools and views in the program. You also learn essential information such as how to open and save a presentation and how to get help.

Sections 4, 5, and 6 get you started building the text portion of a presentation, both by adding text to individual slides in a graphical environment and by entering information into a familiar outline format. You get acquainted with placeholders on slides, which can contain either text or objects, and begin to understand how you build a presentation slide by slide and view the results.

Sections 7, 8, and 9 are where you begin to work with the design aspect of your presentation, using various layouts (different combinations of placeholders and content) and themes that contain color and graphical elements. You work with inserting and manipulating various objects such as clip art, WordArt, and pictures. These chapters also provide valuable information on how to format text and other objects in your presentation so it looks polished and professional.

Section 10 deals with masters, tools that allow you to quickly and easily make changes to global design and text settings that apply to all your slides, handouts, or notes pages.

Sections 11 and 12 take you near to your goal of a final presentation, by providing information about slick animations and transitions that you can add to your slides to bring them to life. You also learn about how to set up your show to run as you wish and how to rehearse, proof, and generally ensure that your presentation is letter perfect.

Sections 13, 14, and 15 help you actually give your presentation to others, either by running it in person, printing out hard copies of it, or publishing it to the Web. This is what all the rest of the work was for, and if you have done your job right, you will be providing a well-written and designed presentation to your audience.

Finally, Section 16 offers information about a few more advanced tools of PowerPoint 2007 that you may want to explore once you've mastered the basics. Among other things, you discover how to work with presentation templates to save you time, collaborate with others in building a presentation, and create custom shows from your larger presentation.

A Few Assumptions

To write a book, you have to first think about your readers. Who are they, what do they already know, and what do they need to know? In writing this book, I've assumed that you are essentially computer literate; you know what a mouse is and how to click and double-click items with it, how to turn your computer on and off, and how to select text or objects. You have also worked with some kind of software and have at least a passing acquaintance with tool buttons, dialog boxes, and software menus of commands.

Whether you use your computer every day in a high-powered job, or spend most of your computer time playing games and writing notes to friends, I assume you've been on the Internet and have an Internet connection. Other than that, this book tries to provide all the steps you need to accomplish the tasks within it in a straightforward way with plenty of graphics to help you see what I'm talking about.

What's New in PowerPoint 2007?

The better question might be what isn't new in PowerPoint 2007? Microsoft Office 2007 products, which include PowerPoint, introduce a powerful new approach to software. Gone are the somewhat redundant toolbars and menus of commands (except for the lone File menu that allows you to open, close, save, and print files and access program options and settings). Choices that used to hide in dialog boxes are in some cases right out in the open through a device called the ribbon.

The ribbon is a central set of tools, divided onto tabs. These tools occasionally offer galleries of choices, and when you move your mouse over those choices, they are previewed on your slides before you apply them. Sometimes when you are working on certain functions specialized tabs will appear; for example, if you select a drawing object, a Drawing Tool Format tab appears.

In addition, contextual tools sometimes pop up. If you select text, for example, a little text formatting toolbar appears right where you're working so common functions such as applying bold or another color to text are quick and easy to do.

A customizable Quick Access toolbar is where you can find a few very common functions such as saving or undoing an action, but you can also add to it any tools you like to work with often.

Finally, PowerPoint 2007 offers more themes and color schemes, more animation effects, and more tools for collaborating on presentations. I think you'll like what you see, once you absorb the changes. PowerPoint 2007 is all about making the tools you work with accessible and obvious.

The Final Word

This book is designed to make your learning painless, with plenty of visual information to help you pick things up with a glance and easy-to-follow steps. My goals were to give you what you need, make it easy to find and understand, and help you have fun learning to work with PowerPoint, which is a great design tool that will help you communicate more effectively.

I hope you find the tasks in this book helpful and that you are producing award-winning presentations in no time.

What's New in PowerPoint 2007?

In this section:

- What's Where in PowerPoint 2007?
- Using the Ribbon
- Working with the Mini Toolbar
- Customizing the Quick Access Toolbar
- Working with New Design Elements

PowerPoint 2007 sports a brand new interface that offers a somewhat different way of getting things done. After investing a little time getting used to the new tools and features, you'll find that this version of PowerPoint is actually easier to use. But if you've used PowerPoint or other Office products before, you have a small learning curve to go through.

This chapter is where you get your first look at PowerPoint 2007, discovering where various tools and settings reside and learning how to use the newest features such as the ribbon and the galleries of design styles.

PowerPoint 2007 has only a single menu, the File menu, which you display by clicking the Office button. Other than the File menu, which offers file management commands such as New, Open, Save, and Print, most features are available as buttons on tabs of the ribbon. In some cases, there are panes that display, such as the Research pane, which are essentially like task panes in PowerPoint 2003.

Galleries of graphic selections allow you to preview how effects will look on your slides or objects before you apply them. Finally, there are a few contextual tools that appear only when needed.

What's Where in PowerPoint 2007?

PowerPoint now uses a central ribbon of tools that you access on various tabs. The tabs include tools broken into groups. In addition, a Quick Access toolbar offers you the ability to place your favorite tools in one location and access functions that aren't offered through the ribbon. Some tools on the ribbon offer drop-down galleries of selections. Some tools open dialog boxes for making detailed settings.

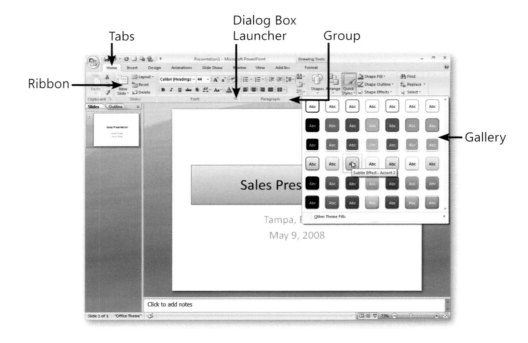

You access the File menu by clicking the Office button. Here you can choose several common file commands or click the PowerPoint Options button to see a wealth of setting options that control the way PowerPoint—and you—work.

Office button

Contextual tab

File menu

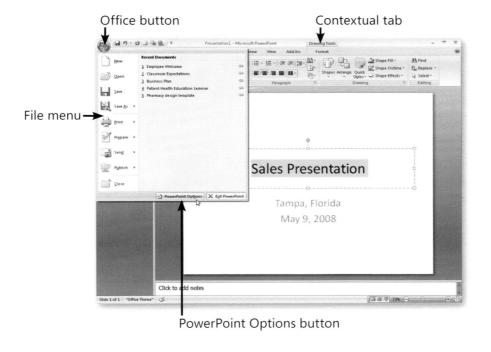

PowerPoint Options button

Using the Ribbon

The ribbon is your control central in PowerPoint 2007. The default ribbon consists of seven tabs, although contextual tabs may appear now and then when working with certain types of objects or functions. An eighth tab, Add-Ins, appears if you install third-party programs and features such as Microsoft PowerPoint Presenter Tools, or a tool like the one I used to capture the screens for this book.

Display Tabs and Panes

① Click the Review tab.

② Click the Research button to open the Research pane.

③ Click the Close button to close the pane.

(continued on the next page)

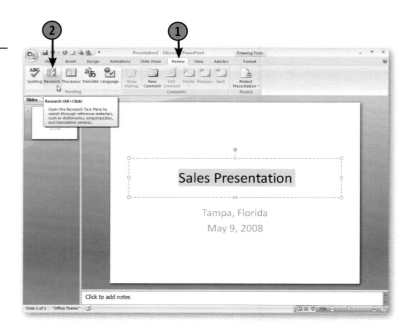

Display Tabs and Panes *(continued)*

4. Click the Insert tab.
5. Click the Shapes button, and then click on an item in the Shapes group. Click and drag anywhere on the slide to draw the shape.
6. Note the Drawing Tools Format tab that appears (this is a contextual tab).

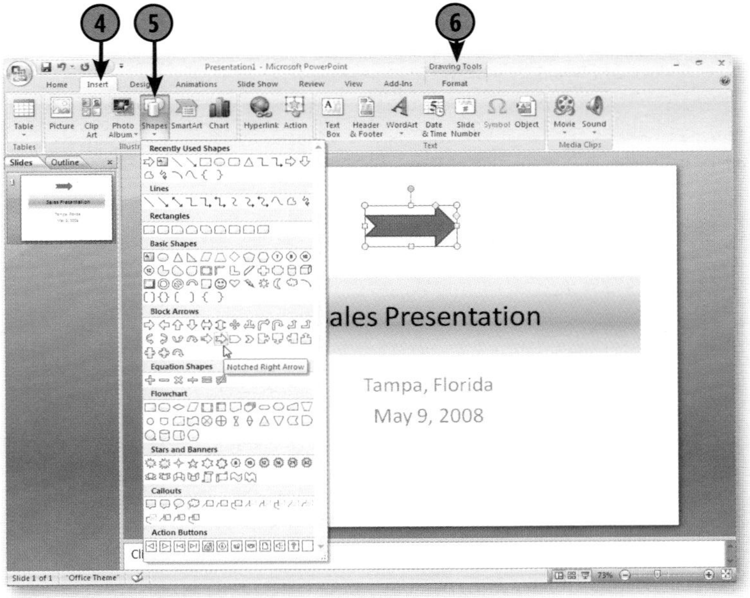

Try This!

You can open dialog boxes associated with groups of tools by clicking the Dialog Box Launcher, a small arrow on the bottom right corner of many groups on the ribbon. This displays additional settings and features related to the ribbon functions.

Tip

The Add-Ins tab is where you can add programs or features that are not part of PowerPoint. You include add-in programs here using the PowerPoint Options in the File menu. For example, there are additional presenter tools or presentation notes tools you can include as add-ins.

Tip

Can't find a tool? Some tools, such as Preview as a Web Page, are not on the ribbon. In that case, you have to add the tools to the Quick Access toolbar to perform the function. See the task Customize the Quick Access Toolbar later in this section for more about how to do this. There is also a helpful listing in PowerPoint Help that tells you how to find the tools you knew in PowerPoint 2003 in their new locations in PowerPoint 2007.

Show or Hide Enhanced ScreenTips

(1) Click the Office button to open the File menu.

(2) Click PowerPoint Options.

(3) Click Popular.

(4) Click the ScreenTip Style drop-down arrow and choose one of the settings:

- Show Feature Descriptions In ScreenTips displays larger ScreenTips with the tool button name and an explanation of its function.

- Don't Show Feature Descriptions In ScreenTips displays only the tool button name.

- Don't Show ScreenTips displays neither enhanced nor standard ScreenTips.

(5) Click OK.

(continued on the next page)

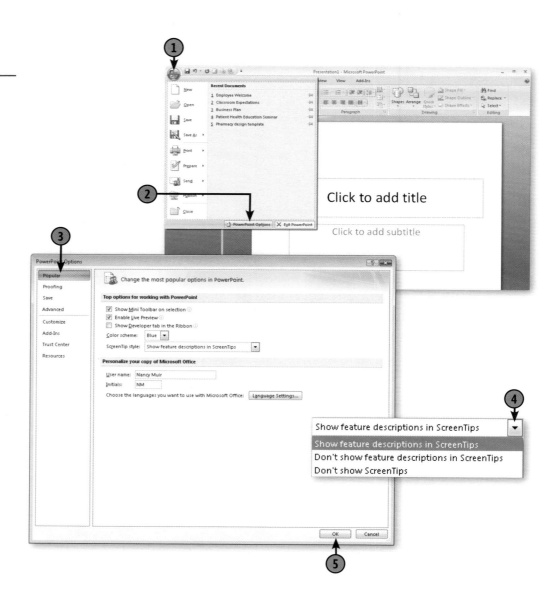

Show or Hide Enhanced ScreenTips *(continued)*

6 Hover your mouse over a button on the ribbon and the appropriate setting takes effect (this shows the Show Feature Descriptions In ScreenTips setting).

When you display either type of ScreenTip, keystroke shortcuts for tool button functions are also displayed, when they exist. So, for example, if you hover your mouse over the Paste button, you will see (Ctrl+V) in parentheses after the tool name in the ScreenTip. You can use this keystroke combination to perform a paste rather than clicking the button, if you wish.

Working with the Mini Toolbar

Anybody who has ever worked on any kind of document, from a word processed letter to a PowerPoint presentation, knows that formatting text is one of the most frequent tasks you perform. That is perhaps why Microsoft added the Mini toolbar in this version of PowerPoint. Now, when you select text, a small floating toolbar appears right next to the text itself. You can easily click on tools such as Bold, Italic, or Font Size without having to move your mouse up to the ribbon and back to the text again.

See Also

For more information about working with text formatting tools that appear both on the Home tab of the ribbon and in the Mini toolbar, see Section 10, "Formatting Text, Objects, and Slides."

Tip

The Mini toolbar is somewhat translucent when you first select text; you have to move your mouse over to it to get a solid image of the tool buttons on it. If you move the mouse away from the toolbar, you have to reselect the text to make it appear again.

Display the Mini Toolbar

① Click the Office button to open the File menu.

② Click PowerPoint Options.

Display the Mini Toolbar *(continued)*

③ Click Popular.

④ Click the Show Mini Toolbar On Selection checkbox.

⑤ Click OK.

⑥ Select text on a slide; the Mini toolbar appears.

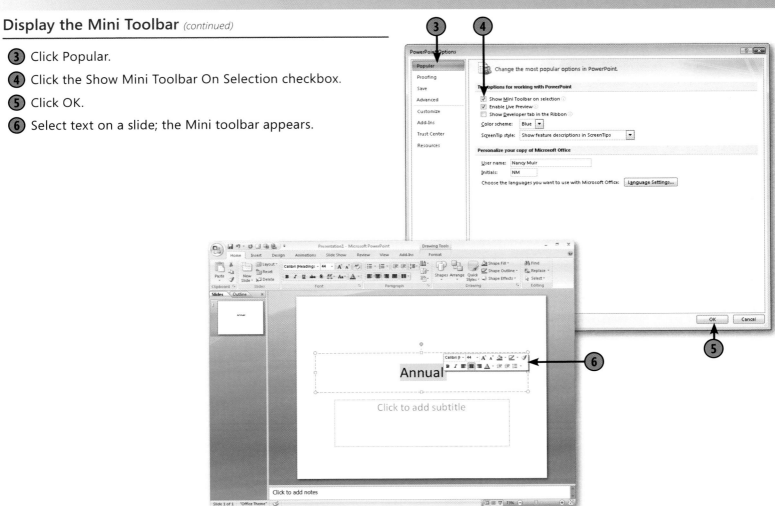

Customizing the Quick Access Toolbar

The idea behind the new interface in Microsoft Office 2007 is that the most commonly used tools are present on the ribbon rather than buried in dialog boxes, and the tools you use less often, though accessible, aren't part of the main interface by default. Sometimes the only way to access a function you may have used in previous versions of PowerPoint is to place a command on the Quick Access toolbar. By default this toolbar contains only the Save, Undo, and Redo commands, but you can add as many commands as you wish.

Add Buttons to the Quick Access Toolbar

 Click the Office button.

2 Click the PowerPoint Options button.

(continued on the next page)

Caution

Although you can add many tools to the toolbar, don't overdo it. Only add the tools you use most often, or add a tool to use a particular function, and then delete it to clear clutter off the toolbar.

Add Buttons to the Quick Access Toolbar *(continued)*

③ Click Customize.

④ Click the arrow on the Choose Commands From drop-down list and select a category of tool, or simply scroll down and choose the Commands Not On the Ribbon category.

⑤ Click on a command in the list on the left and then click the Add button to add it to the toolbar. Repeat this with all tools you wish to add.

⑥ Click OK.

⑦ The tools are added to the toolbar.

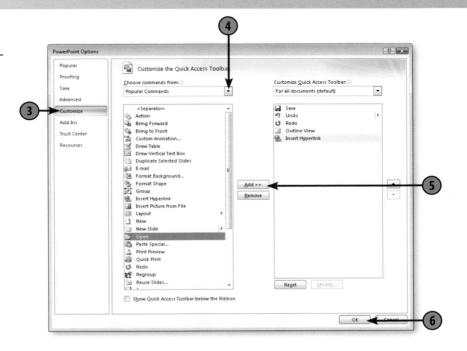

Tip

If you have filled up your Quick Access toolbar and want to put it back the way it was when you first installed PowerPoint, go to the PowerPoint Options, select Customize window and click Reset. The default tool settings are restored.

Remove or Rearrange Tools

① Click the Office button.

② Click the PowerPoint Options button.

(continued on the next page)

Try This!

You can change the Quick Access toolbar settings only for a currently opened document, not for all documents. When you are in the Customize window of PowerPoint Options, click the arrow on the Customize Quick Access Toolbar drop-down box and choose the name of the presentation for which you want to save the changes.

Tip

If you want to add some space between sets of tools on the tool bar, simply click on the item labeled <Separator> at the top of the list on the left of the Customize window and click Add.

Remove or Rearrange
Tools *(continued)*

(3) Click Customize.

(4) Click an item in the list on the right.

(5) Click Remove to remove it from the toolbar.

(6) Click Move Up or Move Down to rearrange the tools.

(7) Click OK to save your settings.

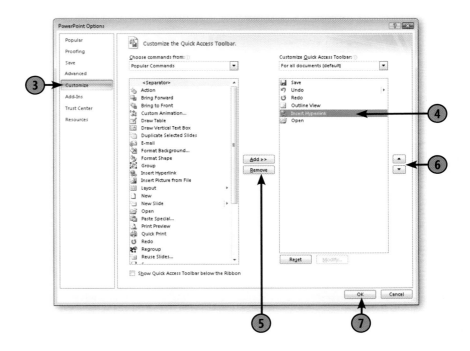

Working with New Design Elements

Several new features in PowerPoint 2007 relate to how graphics are displayed and created. Galleries of graphic elements help you browse through different styles and preview how each will look in your presentation. Themes and Quick Styles are designed to give your presentation a cohesive and consistent look with predesigned combinations of colors, graphics, and fonts. Finally, SmartArt is a new feature that allows you to easily create various types of diagrams and add text to them.

Preview Design Elements with Galleries

① Click a placeholder on a slide, enter some text, and select the text.

② Click the Format tab.

③ Click the More arrow along the right of the WordArt Styles gallery.

④ Move your mouse over various WordArt styles. You will be able to see each style previewed on the selected text. Click a style to apply it.

(continued on the next page)

Tip

Several galleries exist on tabs that don't appear until you insert certain types of objects, such as pictures or drawings. There is also a Shapes gallery on the Insert tab you can use to draw shapes on your slides.

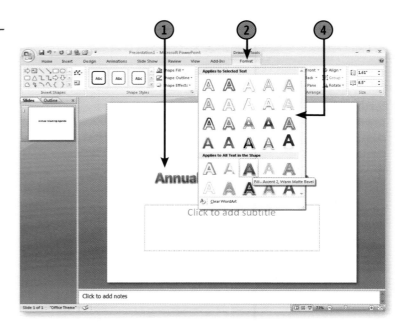

Preview Design Elements with Galleries *(continued)*

(5) Click the Home tab and click the arrow on the Font field.

(6) Move your mouse down the list of fonts. You will be able to see each font previewed on the selected text. Click a font to apply it.

Try This!

You can preview font sizes on selected text. With text selected, click the arrow on the Font Size field and move your mouse down the list of sizes. Each is previewed on your text.

See Also

For more information about WordArt and other drawing objects, see Section 9.

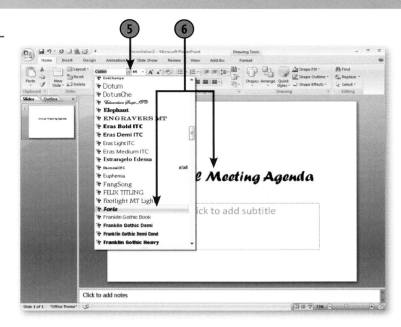

Get a Cohesive Look with Themes

① Click the Design tab.

② Click the More arrow to the right of the Themes gallery. The gallery appears.

③ Move your mouse over the various themes. You will see each one previewed on your slide presentation.

④ Click a theme to apply it your entire presentation.

(continued on the next page)

Try This!

You can modify a theme by selecting a different color, font, or effect set on the Design tab. You will find that even if you experiment with different combinations, by using these preset design elements you can keep consistency in the various design features of your slides.

See Also

For more information about working with themes and other design elements, see Section 7.

Get a Cohesive Look with Themes *(continued)*

5 Click the Colors button and move your mouse over the sets of colors to see them previewed on your slides. Click a theme to apply it.

Themes are new to PowerPoint 2007, and you can expand your Theme horizons by using the More Themes on Microsoft Office Online link at the bottom of the Theme Gallery. Office Online offers additional looks for your presentation that can give it extra visual excitement.

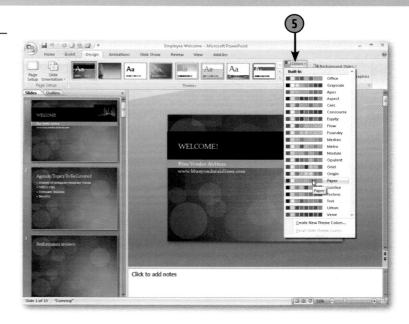

Work with SmartArt

1 Click the Insert tab.

2 Click the SmartArt button to open the Choose a SmartArt Graphic dialog box.

3 Click on a category of SmartArt in the list on the left.

4 Click an item in the gallery of SmartArt to select it.

5 Click OK. The SmartArt object appears on the slide.

6 Click in the Type Your Text Here box and type your text.

Tip

Look at the preview of SmartArt in the Choose a SmartArt Graphic dialog box. Beneath it is a suggestion of uses for that particular SmartArt element to best communicate your message.

See Also

See Section 8 for more about working with SmartArt objects as well as tables and various kinds of drawn objects.

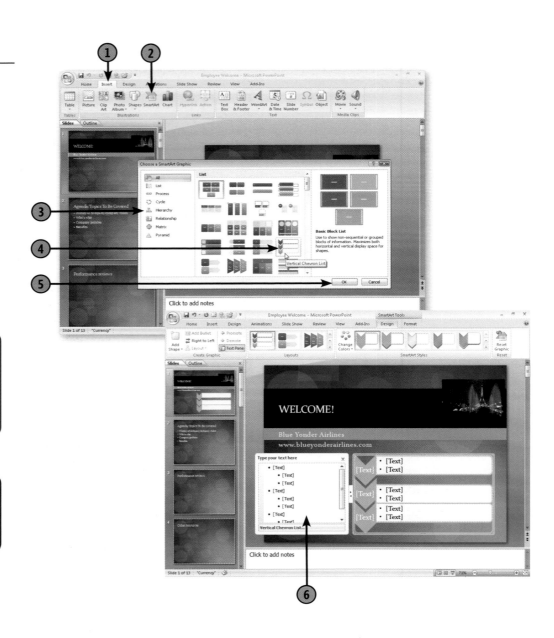

Getting Started with PowerPoint 2007

In this section:

- Creating a New Blank or Template-Based Presentation
- Finding and Opening Existing Presentations
- Sizing Panes in Normal View
- Viewing Multiple Slides with Slide Sorter
- Running a Presentation in Slide Show View
- Saving and Closing a PowerPoint Presentation
- Getting Help

When you start a new job, you typically spend the first day getting acquainted with colleagues and finding your way around the office before you get to work. In the same way, whether you want to create a lengthy, elaborate animated presentation with sound and graphics or a simple bullet list presentation consisting of a handful of slides, your first step is to learn how to open a blank presentation and the basic structure of a typical PowerPoint presentation.

You can open a blank presentation, open presentations you have previously created and saved, or create new presentations based on templates that provide prebuilt design features. After you open a file, you can enter content for a presentation. Then, if you've made changes, you need to know how to save those changes and close the presentation.

As you wander around PowerPoint, you get to know the different views that you will use depending on what you want to accomplish. When you open a presentation, it opens in Normal view, where you see three panes containing a slide/outline display, the current slide, and an area for notes.

The Slide Sorter view is where you go to organize slides. When you want to see your show in action, use the Slide Show view.

Creating a New Presentation

PowerPoint offers you a few options for how you get started with a new presentation. For example, if you want a single blank slide with the default layout and design elements, you can open a blank presentation. But if you'd like to get a head start on your presentation, consider opening it either based on an existing presentation that contains some elements you want to reuse or applying one of PowerPoint's predesigned templates.

Open a Blank Presentation

1 With PowerPoint running, click the Office button to open the File menu and choose New to display the New Presentation window.

2 Double-click Blank Presentation to open a new presentation based on the blank template.

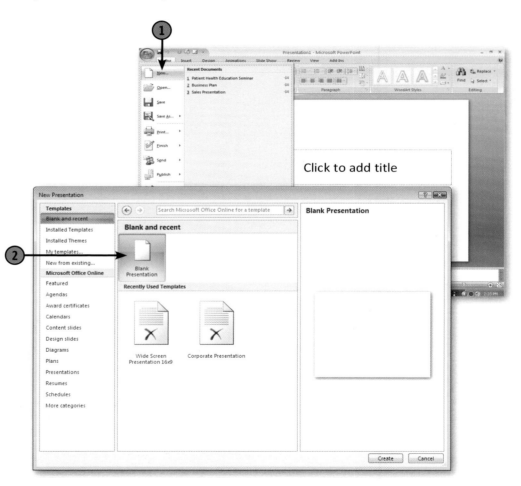

Tip

If you're more comfortable using a keyboard shortcut to open a new file, you can. Simply press Ctrl+O to display the Open dialog box or Ctrl+N to open a new, blank presentation. You should note, however, that keyboard shortcuts are no longer displayed on the File menu in PowerPoint 2007. You have to hover your mouse over a command to see any keyboard shortcut. All shortcuts that start with Ctrl are the same as in PowerPoint 2003; however, some that began with Alt have changed.

Open a Presentation Based on an Existing Presentation

1. With PowerPoint running, click the Office button and in the File menu click New to display the New Presentation window.

2. Click New From Existing.

3. Click the down arrow to browse the drives and folders of your computer or network to locate a file.

4. Double-click a folder to open it and display files. Continue to double-click folders until you find the file you want.

5. Click the document file to select it.

6. Click Open to open a new presentation based on the selected existing presentation.

See Also

For information about saving files, see "Saving and Closing a PowerPoint Presentation" on page 34.

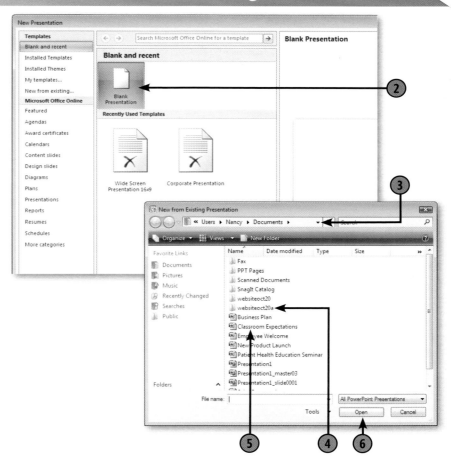

Tip

Be sure to save the file you have just opened with a new name to preserve its contents. Saving it with a name different from the existing file it is based on ensures that you don't overwrite the original file.

Open a Template

(1) With PowerPoint running, click the Office button and choose New from the menu to display the New Presentation window.

(2) If you are online, you can click a template category on the left side of the New Presentation window to display thumbnails of templates available from Office Online in that category.

(3) Click Installed Templates to view templates installed on your computer when you installed PowerPoint.

(4) Click a template to see a preview and information about it on the right side of the window. In some cases, clicking a category displays a list of subcategories; click one to view template thumbnails.

(5) Click a template to select it and then click Download.

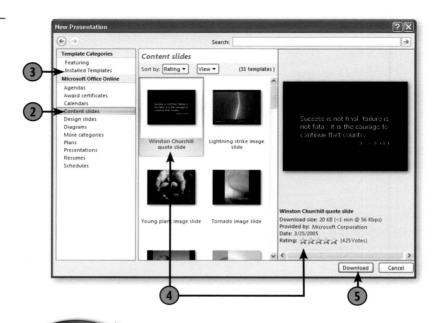

Tip

Many of the categories you see in the New Presentation window are accessed from Office Online. If you're working offline you'll have to use an installed template, theme, or templates you have created and saved on your computer.

See Also

Note that any template you apply to your presentation will then be accessible by clicking Themes on the Design tab. For information about applying themes to slides, see "Apply a Slide Theme" on page 80.

Finding and Opening Existing Presentations

Very often it takes several work sessions to complete a presentation. Perhaps you'll enter slide text in one sitting, tweak the arrangement of graphics and colors in another, and still later edit what you've created to incorporate others' feedback or to proof for spelling errors. To open an existing presentation, you can use the following steps.

Open a Presentation

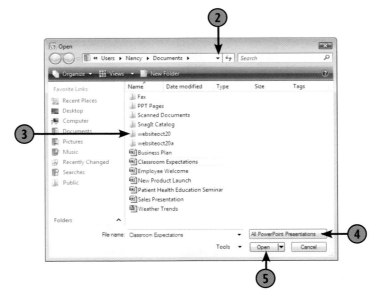

1. With PowerPoint running, click the Office button and choose Open from the File menu to display the Open dialog box.

2. Click the down arrow to browse the drives and folders of your computer or network to locate a file.

3. Double-click a folder to open it and display files. Continue to double-click folders until you find the file you want.

4. Specify the file type for the document you want to locate; All PowerPoint Presentations is the default format. Only documents saved in the specified file format are displayed in the file list.

5. Click on a file and then click the Open button to open it.

Tip

You can use the buttons along the left of the Open dialog box to find a file more quickly. For example, if you used the file recently, click the Recently Changed button; if the file is stored in a shared folder on a network, click the Public button to locate it, and so on.

Tip

In PowerPoint 2003, recently used files were listed at the bottom of the File menu. In the newly designed File menu, which you access from the Office button in PowerPoint 2007, recently used files are listed to the right of the menu commands. Just click on one of these to open it.

Moving among Views

PowerPoint 2007 offers four views that let you focus on different aspects of your presentation. Three of the views, Normal, Slide Sorter, and Slide Show, can be accessed from buttons on the taskbar located along the bottom of your screen; the fourth, Notes Page, is accessed through the View tab. Note that these buttons do not appear when you are in Slide Show view; you must exit the Slide Show to use them. You learn more about how each view is used in the following sections.

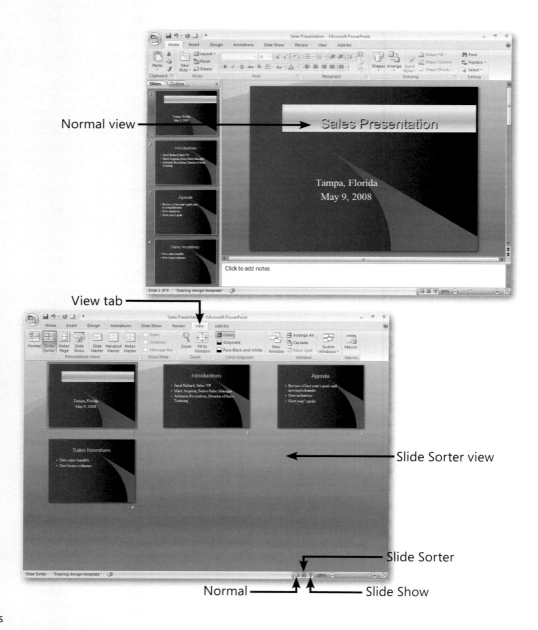

Normal view

View tab

Slide Sorter view

Slide Sorter

Normal

Slide Show

Slide Show view

Sizing Panes in Normal View

You will do most of your work building your presentation in Normal view. It consists of three panes: the Slides/Outline pane gives you access to tabs that provide an overview of your presentation; the Notes pane is where you enter speaker notes to help you when you are giving your presentation; and the Slide pane is where you work on the design of an individual slide. You can temporarily remove the Slides/Outline or Notes panes, or you can resize them to focus on one aspect of your presentation.

Resize a Pane

① Move your mouse over the edge of the Slides/Outline or Notes pane until the cursor turns into two lines with double arrows.

② Click and drag in the appropriate direction to make the pane larger or smaller.

If you drag a pane divider until the pane disappears, the divider will still be visible so that you can click and drag the divider to redisplay the pane.

You can change how large the slide preview appears in the Slide pane without resizing the pane by clicking and dragging the Zoom slider at the bottom of the PowerPoint screen. To refit the slide to the Slide pane in Normal view after you've changed its zoom setting, you can click the Fit Slide to Current Window button, located to the right of the slider. Note that the Fit Slide to Current Window button does not appear in any other view.

Close and Redisplay the Slides/ Outline Pane

① Click the Close button on the Slides/Outline pane to hide it.

② Click the Normal button to redisplay the pane.

See Also

For information about working with the Slides tab, see "Building a Presentation" on page 37.

For information about working with the Outline feature, see "Building a Presentation Outline" on page 53.

Try This!

Take advantage of the ability to hide and resize panes to make your work easier. If you are focused on slide design rather than on entering slide text, close or make the Slides/Outline pane smaller. If you want to quickly enter text in an outline format for many slides, enlarge the Slides/ Outline pane to make the Outline tab larger and the text easier to read.

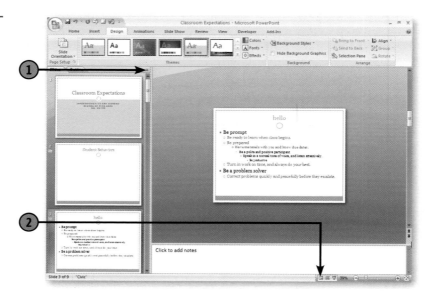

Viewing Multiple Slides with Slide Sorter

After you have created several slides, you may want to take your focus off individual slides and look at your presentation as a whole. The best view for this task is Slide Sorter view, which displays all your slides as thumbnails placed in sequence from left to right. If you have many slides, they will be arranged in rows. In this view, it's easy to rearrange slides to organize your show and to duplicate or delete slides.

Display Slide Sorter View

 Click the Slide Sorter button to display the view.

To return to Normal view from Slide Sorter and display a particular slide, just double-click that slide's thumbnail in Slide Sorter. Normal view opens with the selected slide displayed in the Slide pane.

Notice that certain tabs of the ribbon, such as Insert and Design, have most or all of their commands unavailable in Slide Sorter. That's because Slide Sorter is not the view you use to work on slide content. Rather, you use it to organize slides. To work on slide content, you have to return to Normal view where the tools on those tabs will be available to you.

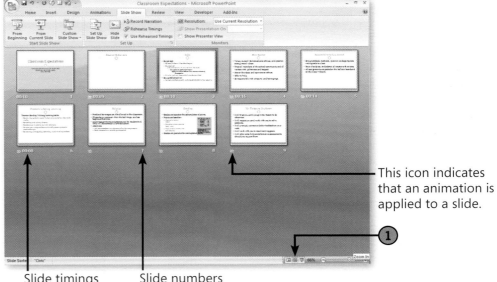

This icon indicates that an animation is applied to a slide.

Slide timings appear beneath slides if you have rehearsed the presentation and saved timings.

Slide numbers are displayed beneath each slide.

Display More Slides in Slide Sorter

1. Click the slider on the Zoom tool.

2. Drag to the left to make the thumbnails smaller, thereby fitting more slides on the screen. Drag to the right to make thumbnails bigger, fitting fewer on a screen.

See Also

You can do more than view slides in Slide Sorter view. You can delete, duplicate, hide, and reorder slides, as well as preview animations and more. See "Managing and Viewing Slides" on page 65 for more features of this handy view.

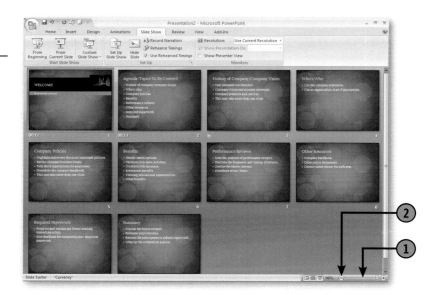

Running a Presentation in Slide Show View

Slide Show is the view you use to run your presentation in full screen mode. If you have your computer connected to an LCD or television monitor, your audience can view in a larger screen format what you see on your computer screen.

Slide Show view has several useful tools for navigating through your show, including a pen feature that lets you annotate your slides as you are showing them. You can even save your annotations at the end of the show.

Start a Slide Show and Advance Slides

1 Click the Slide Show view button to display the slide show starting with the currently selected slide.

2 Click the left arrow on your keyboard to move back one slide; click the right arrow on your keyboard to move forward one slide.

End a Slide Show

1 With a presentation in Slide Show view, press Escape on your keyboard to end the slide show and return to the view you had displayed when you started the presentation (Normal or Slide Sorter).

2 If you have created any annotations while running the show, a dialog box appears asking whether you want to save your annotations. Click Keep or Discard.

Tip

You can end a slide show at any point, whether you've reached the last slide or not, using the method provided here. If, however, you finish running through the slides in your show and reach the end, you will see a message that the show is over; if you see that message, you can then press any key to close the slide show.

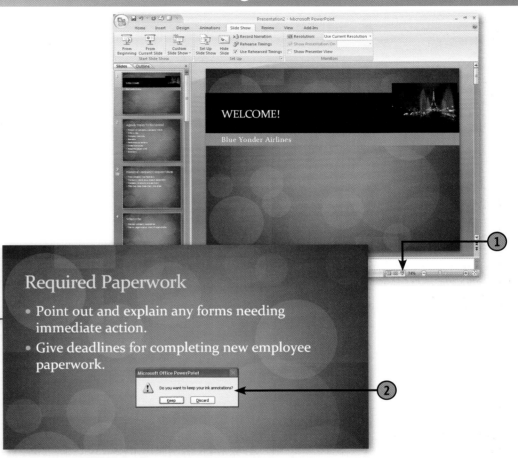

See Also

For information about using different methods to navigate through a slide show, including your mouse, on screen buttons, and the Slide Show menu, see "Running a Presentation" on page 187. For information about setting up the way a slide show will run, see "Finalizing Your Slide Show" on page 171.

Saving and Closing a PowerPoint Presentation

When you have worked on a presentation for a while, you should save it periodically so you don't run the risk of losing any of your work in the case of a computer crash or other problem. You should also save any changes before closing a file.

Save a Presentation

 Click the Office button and choose Save from the File menu to display the Save As dialog box.

(continued on the next page)

(continued on the next page)

Try This!

If you want to save a previously saved presentation with a new name, perhaps to use as the basis for another presentation, you can choose Save As from the File menu. Enter a new filename and, if you wish, locate another folder in which to save the file. Click Save, and you have saved a copy of the presentation with a new name.

Tip

To quickly save any changes to a previously saved document, simply click the Save button on the Quick Access bar. The file is saved with all previous save settings, without displaying the Save As dialog box.

Tip

You can now save a presentation in XML format, which compresses the file to make it easy to share online. Simply choose Save As, Other Format from the File menu in Step 4 of this task to use this feature.

Save a Presentation *(continued)*

2 If you don't want to save the presentation to the default folder, select another drive or folder.

3 Type a name for the document of up to 255 characters; you cannot use the characters * : < > | " \ or /.

4 To save the document in a format other than the default PowerPoint file format (ppt), select a different format.

5 Click Save.

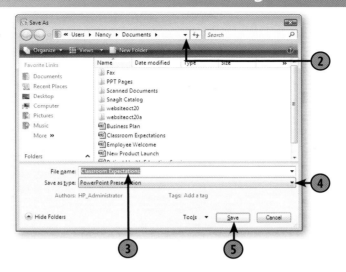

Close a Presentation

1 Click the Save button to be sure all changes have been saved.

2 Click the Close button to close the file and PowerPoint.

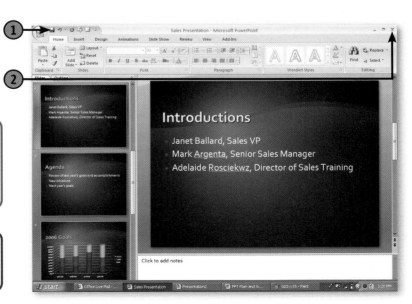

Try This!

If you want to close an open presentation without closing PowerPoint—for example, to begin on a new, blank presentation—click the Office button and choose Close from the File menu.

Tip

You can also close PowerPoint by choosing Exit PowerPoint from the Office menu.

Getting Help

PowerPoint 2007 includes both offline help, in the form of a searchable database of information, and online help that takes you to a Microsoft Web site. Learning how to use PowerPoint Help will enable you to solve small problems that you run into and delve deeper into PowerPoint features.

Use Help

1. Click the Help button to display the Microsoft Office PowerPoint Help window.

2. Choose the kind of help you want to search.

3. Click the Show Table Of Contents button for a list of offline help topics.

4. Click Home to go to the main listing of topics at any time.

5. Click the Print button to print the currently displayed topic.

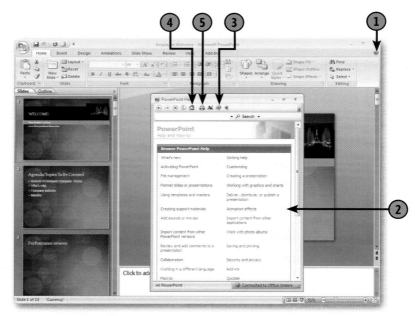

Caution

If you want to keep the window available as you work in your document, click the Keep On Top button in the Help window before clicking within the document.

Tip

Often Help search results will include links to other information. These links appear in blue. Click on one, and you are taken to a Web page or other document where you can find related or additional information.

Building a Presentation

In this section:

- Understanding How to Build a Presentation
- Building a Slide
- Working with Text
- Finding and Replacing Text
- Manipulating Placeholders

Although a presentation can contain text, graphics, animations, and special elements such as charts and WordArt, most presentations begin with you entering some kind of text. Text is used for the major headings of each slide as well as for the individual bullet points that provide the details of your topic. You can enter text in an outline (see section 5 for more about this) or in placeholders on individual slides in the Normal view of PowerPoint.

In this section you discover how to insert a new slide in your presentation and enter text on it. Once you have entered text, you will typically need to edit it by modifying what you've entered, cutting or copying text and then pasting it in new locations, or finding and replacing text. As you insert and edit text, knowing how to undo and redo actions as you go is another useful skill you'll be very glad to have, and it's covered in this chapter, too.

Finally in this chapter, you work with manipulating the placeholders where you enter text. You can apply formatting to placeholders and align the text within them. One other feature that is new to PowerPoint 2007 is the Selection and Visibility pane, which aides you in selecting and manipulating placeholders on slides.

Understanding How to Build a Presentation

You enter most text, as well as other elements such as pictures and tables, by using placeholders on slides in Normal view. Slide title and subtitle placeholders typically hold a single heading, while content placeholders are usually used for a bulleted list of key points. When you enter text in placeholders, it is reflected in the Outline tab in Normal view. You can format placeholders to use fill colors and borders.

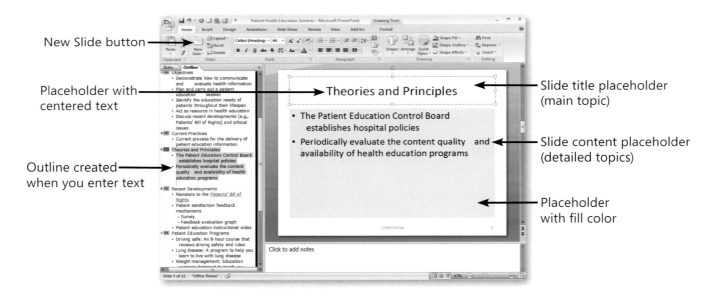

New Slide button

Placeholder with centered text

Outline created when you enter text

Slide title placeholder (main topic)

Slide content placeholder (detailed topics)

Placeholder with fill color

Building a Slide

When you open a blank presentation, PowerPoint provides you with one blank title slide. A title slide contains two placeholders, a title and a subtitle. When you insert a slide, a title and content slide is inserted by default. This contains a title placeholder where you enter the topic for the slide and a placeholder for inserting bulleted points for that topic. There are other slide layouts that use text placeholders, but for building presentation contents, these are the two types of slides you will use most often. (See section 9 for information about working with slide layouts that include graphic elements).

Insert a New Slide

① Click the Home tab.

② Click the New Slide button to insert a new title and content slide.

③ Click the arrow on the New Slide button and click another option from the Office Theme drop-down box to insert a slide with a different layout.

There are other text-only slide layouts as well as a blank slide. Try inserting a Section Header or a Two Content slide layout from the Layout drop-down list. You can add text to a blank slide by using a text box (see "Add a Text Box" on page 122), although text in a text box is not reflected in the presentation outline.

Although this section deals with the basics of inserting slides with a few different layouts, I deal with different slide layouts in more detail in Section 7.

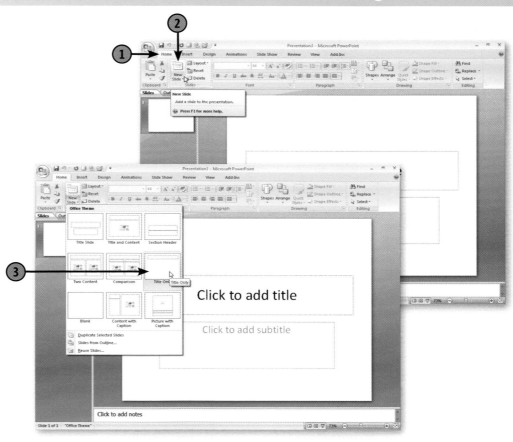

The Comparison slide layout includes a title placeholder, two subtitle placeholders, and two content placeholders. If you want to display two lists side by side with a heading to describe the contents of each, this is a useful layout to use.

Enter Text on Slides

1 Click a Title placeholder.

2 Type your text and then click anywhere outside the placeholder.

3 Click a Content placeholder and type one line of text, then press Enter and type the next line of text. Bullet points are added automatically.

Tip

You can modify bullet point styles that are inserted in content placeholders. Click the arrow on the Bullets button in the Paragraph group of the Home tab and choose a different style or click Bullets and Numbering at the bottom of the list to customize bullet styles.

See Also

For information about formatting text you type into placeholders, see "Formatting Text" on page 126.

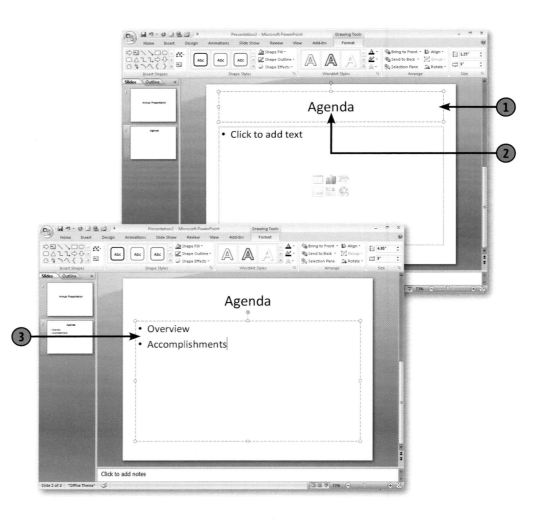

Insert a Symbol

(1) Click in a placeholder where you want to insert a symbol.

(2) Click the Insert tab.

(3) Click the Symbol button.

(4) Click the arrow on the Font field to choose a font set.

(5) Scroll to locate the symbol you want to insert and click on it.

(6) Click Insert. The symbol is inserted on the slide.

(7) Continue to locate and insert symbols you need and click Close when you're done.

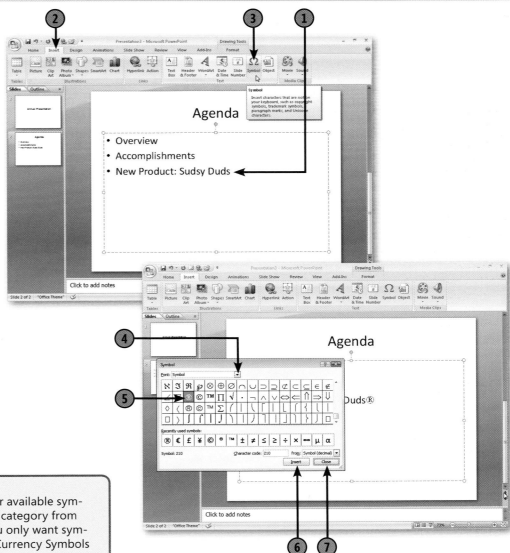

Tip

All fonts have some symbols such as percent and dollar signs, but if you're looking for little pictures or design elements rather than text, your best bet is to choose from these font sets: Symbol, Wingding, Wingding 2 or 3, or Webdings.

Try This!

For some Font sets you can narrow down your available symbols in the Symbols dialog box by choosing a category from the Subset drop-down list. For example, if you only want symbols for international currencies, choose the Currency Symbols category, and if you only want arrow symbols choose Arrows.

Insert the Date and Time

1. Click the placeholder where you want to insert the date and time.
2. Click the Insert tab.
3. Click the Date and Time button.
4. Click a date and time format.
5. Click OK.

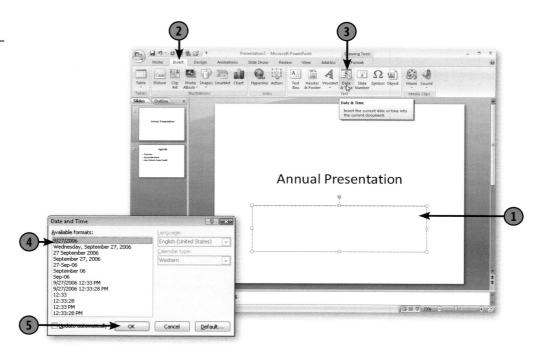

Try This!

If you want the date and time to update every time you print or show your presentation, click the Update Automatically checkbox in the Date and Time dialog box before you click OK.

Tip

You can also place the date and time in a footer on a slide master so it will appear on every slide in your presentation. See Section 10 for more about working with masters.

Working with Text

Most of us aren't letter perfect the first time we write something. We need to go back and make changes and even undo some things we've done. Sometimes we need to move some text from one spot to another. To help us out, PowerPoint makes it easy to shift things around when we change our minds. We can edit text; cut, copy, and paste text; and undo or redo actions.

For information about cutting, copying, and pasting entire slides or duplicating slide contents, see "Managing and Viewing Slides" on page 65.

The Paste Special command allows you to paste text or objects that you cut or copy into your PowerPoint presentation in different formats, such as HTML, which is readable by Web browsers, or OLE (object linking and embedding), which pastes an icon rather than the actual content in your presentation. For more about working with a presentation outline, see "Working with the Outline" on page 54.

Edit Text

1. Click in a placeholder at the location in the text that you want to edit (note that if you select text to edit it, a Mini toolbar containing formatting tools appears).

2. Take any of the following actions:

   - Press Delete to delete text to the right of the blinking cursor one character at a time.

   - Press Backspace to delete text to the left of the b linking cursor one character at a time.

   - Click and drag over text and press Delete to delete all selected text.

   - Begin typing any additional or replacement text.

3. Click outside the placeholder.

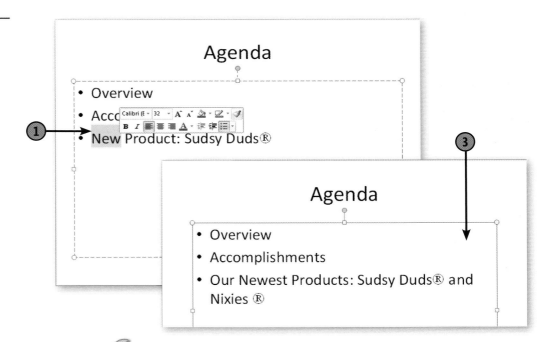

You can also edit text in the Outline pane. Remember that any change you make to placeholder text on a slide is reflected in the outline and vice versa. See Section 5 for more about working with a presentation outline.

Undo and Redo an Action

① After performing an action such as typing, formatting, or moving an object, click the Undo [Action] button on the Quick Access tool-bar. The action is reversed.

② To redo an undone action, click the Redo [Action] button.

③ If you want to undo a series of actions, click the arrow on the Undo [Action] button and choose the actions from the list that appears.

Caution

You can't undo an action you took prior to other actions with-out undoing every action you performed leading up to it. In that case, it may be simplest to just make the change yourself by retyping, reformatting, or whatever it was you did that you want undone.

Tip

A quick and easy way to undo what you've just done is to press Ctrl+Z. You can redo what you've undone by pressing Ctrl+Y.

Cut, Copy, and Paste Text

(1) Click the Home tab.

(2) Click the placeholder you want to copy, or click and drag to select text if you want to copy or cut and paste the text only (and not the placeholder).

(3) Click the Cut or Copy button.

(4) Click where you want to paste the cut or copied text.

(5) Click the Paste button.

Tip

If you click the arrow on the Paste button you can choose to paste an item as a hyperlink, or use the Paste Special command to open the Paste Special dialog box, where you can choose among additional formats.

Tip

You can quickly create a duplicate of a placeholder and its contents by selecting the placeholder and choosing Duplicate from the Paste button drop-down menu.

Finding and Replacing Text

Often when creating a presentation you need to change every instance of a word or phrase. For example, your company might change the name of a product under development. In that case, manually finding and editing each instance can be time consuming. Use the Find and Replace feature to easily find every instance and change them all instantly or one by one.

Find and Replace Text

1 Click the Home tab.

2 Click the Find button.

3 Enter a word or phrase you want to find and change.

4 Click the Replace button.

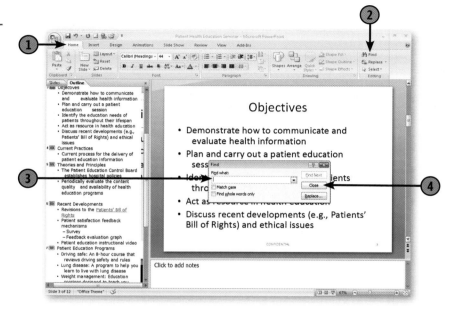

(5) Enter the word or phrase with which you want to replace the original text.

(6) Do one of the following:

■ Click the Find Next button to find the next instance of the text.

■ Click Replace to replace the currently selected instance of the text.

■ Click Replace All to replace all instances of the text.

(7) When you have completed finding or replacing text, a confirming message appears. Click OK.

Tip

Use the Match Case and Find Whole Words Only checkboxes in the Find and Replace dialog box to narrow your search. If, for instance, you want to find the word Bell (a last name) and you don't want lowercase instances of the word bell or words such as bellow, you could use both of these qualifiers for your find and replace operation.

Manipulating Placeholders

With the exception of text boxes (covered in Section 9) place-holders are where you create the elements of your presentation. They contain text, drawings, pictures, charts, and more. Placeholders provide an easy way to arrange the components of each slide, and because they come with certain predesigned formatting, they make adding everything from a bulleted list to a chart easy. By selecting a placeholder (made easier with the new Selection and Visibility pane in PowerPoint 2007), you can align the contents of placeholders and format their backgrounds and borders.

Use the Selection and Visibility Pane

(1) Display the slide you want to work on in Normal view and click the Home tab on the ribbon.

(2) Click the Select button in the Editing group and choose Selection Pane.

(continued on the next page)

Tip

In addition to the Selection and Visibility task pane to help you select objects, you can click the Arrange button on the Home tab and use the Bring to Front and Send to Back buttons to push a selected item in a stack of items to be in front of or in back of others.

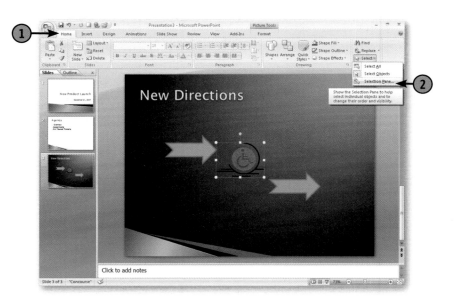

Use the Selection and
Visibility Pane *(continued)*

③ In the Selection and Visibility task pane that appears, do any of the following:

- Click on an item in the list of Shapes On This Slide to select the object.

- Click the Visibility button to hide any item.

- Click the Visibility button again to display the item.

Tip

If you click on an object, the Format tab appears on the ribbon. This tab also contains the Arrange group of tools, including the Selection Pane, Bring to Front, and Send to Back buttons.

See Also

For more information about working with objects on your slides, see Section 9.

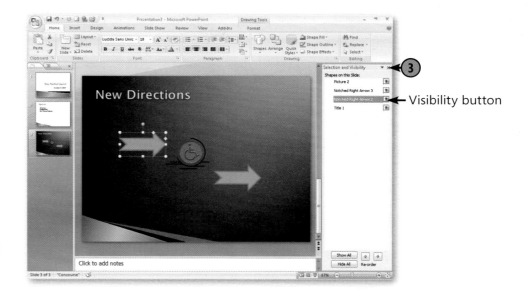

Visibility button

Align Placeholder Contents

(1) Click on the placeholder containing the text you want to align and click the Home tab.

(2) If you only want to align one line of several, select the text you want to align.

(3) Click any of the alignment buttons, and the text shifts accordingly.

Caution

Themes that you apply to your slides provide a certain design balance to elements on the page. Be sure that if you shift the alignment of text in placeholders that the text is balanced on the slide against any graphics or master elements such as footers.

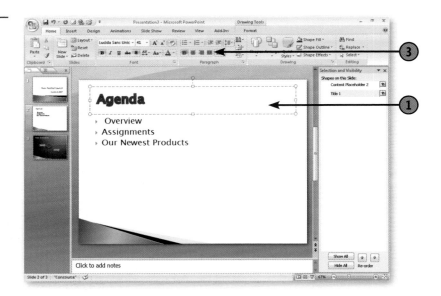

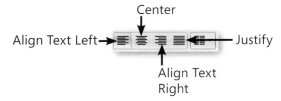

Center

Align Text Left →⬛ ⬛ ⬛ ⬛ ⬛← Justify

Align Text Right

Tip

Use centered text for emphasis for a single line of text. If working with bulleted lists, typically you should use left or justified alignment so each bulleted item begins at the same place, making the list easier to follow.

Formatting Placeholders

1 Right-click the placeholder and choose Format Shape from the shortcut menu.

2 Click a category on the left.

3 Choose settings to add fill color, add and adjust a border line, or add a shadow or 3-D effect. Notice that whatever settings you make are previewed on the placeholder.

4 Click Close to apply your new settings.

Caution

Don't go overboard adding effects to placeholders, especially if your slide contains a lot of graphics and text. Let the text be the important element on any slide to help get your message across.

Tip

After you have applied a fill color to a placeholder, a quick way to change the fill color is to click the Colors button on the Design tab and choose a new color scheme for the presentation.

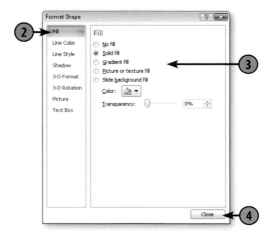

Building a Presentation Outline

5

In this section:

- Understanding the Relationship of the Outline to Slides
- Working with the Outline
- Adding Text in the Outline Tab
- Working with Outline Contents

A tool for organizing your thoughts and information that has been around for quite some time is the outline. An outline breaks down information into multiple headings and subheading levels.

The outlining feature in PowerPoint helps you use this valuable tool to enter text, reorganize it into topics and subtopics, and reorder the contents of your presentation.

You access the outlining feature from the Outline tab in the Slides/Outline pane in Normal view. If you are focused on entering a lot of text and not so much on the look of individual slides, it can be faster to enter that text in the Outline tab rather than through the Slide pane.

When you enter text on a slide, the content is reflected in the outline and vice versa. As you work in the outline, the slide that corresponds to the text you're working on appears in the Slide pane, so you can see how changes to the outline affect the slide.

Another nice aspect of the outlining feature in PowerPoint is that you can display an Outline view that looks much like an outline in a word processor. You can also send an outline to a Word document where it can form the basis of a written presentation or a useful audience handout.

Understanding the Relationship of the Outline to Slides

Different slide layouts contain different placeholders, such as title, subtitle, text, and content placeholders. You can enter text in the placeholders on a slide or in the Outline tab of the Slides/Outline pane. When you enter text into title, subtitle, or text placeholders in the Slide pane, it also appears in the outline. When you enter a top-level heading in the outline, PowerPoint creates a new slide and that heading appears in the slide title placeholder. Any text that you enter at an indented level in the Outline pane becomes bullet points in a text placeholder on the slide.

Note that graphics do not appear in the outline. Text that you enter in text boxes (which are different from text placeholders) also doesn't appear in the outline.

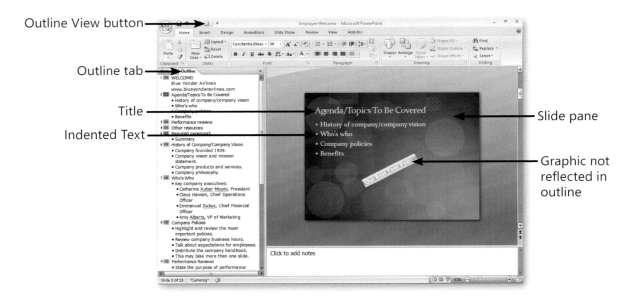

Outline View button

Outline tab

Title

Indented Text

Slide pane

Graphic not reflected in outline

Working with the Outline

You can work on an outline in the Outline tab in the Slides/Outline pane displayed to the left of the Slide pane in Normal view. The Outline tab allows you to compare the outline with slides, which may have graphics or text boxes that don't show up in the outline. Entering text in the outline can be faster than entering it on individual slides when you are purely focused on presentation text contents.

Display the Outline Tab

① Click the Normal view button.

② Click the Outline tab.

③ There is an outline you can display by placing the Outline View icon on the Quick Access toolbar and Clicking it.

Try This!

If you have a long presentation and you display Outline view, the font may be too small to work with. Click and drag the Zoom slider in the bottom right corner of the PowerPoint screen to quickly enlarge the font size of your outline. Note that if you do this while in Normal view with the Outline tab and Slide pane showing, the slide text, but not the outline text, enlarges.

See Also

You can format text in both the Outline tab and the Slide pane to change the size or type. A change made in one place is reflected in the other. For more about changing text format, see "Formatting Text" on page 126.

Tip

What if you want to see a thumbnail of the slide but need more room to work in the outline? You can expand the Outline tab so that it fills about three-quarters of the screen, which leaves you with a small preview of the slide in the Slide pane and large, easy-to-read outline contents. To expand the Outline tab, click on the divider between the Outline tab and Slide pane and drag it to the right as far as you can.

Adding Text in the Outline Tab

One of the benefits of the Outline tab is that it provides a fast way for you to enter text without having to deal with placeholders or graphics. Adding text here consists of entering the text, which appears at the same outline level as the line before.

You can then demote text to become a subheading (subtitle or bullet points) or promote a bullet point to become the next slide title.

Add a Slide Title

① Open a new, blank presentation.

② With the Outline tab selected in Normal view, click in the outline.

③ Enter some text, which will automatically be formatted as the slide title, and press Enter. The slide title appears in both the outline and the Slide pane, and your cursor is in place to create the next slide title.

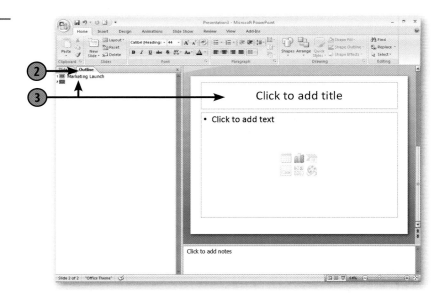

Tip

The first slide is always created using the Title Slide layout. There is typically only one title slide in a presentation, although you could duplicate it and place the duplicate at the end of your presentation. A Title Slide consists of a Title and Subtitle. After the first slide, all other slides you create use the Title and Content layout by default.

See Also

For more information about slide layouts, see "What Slide Layouts and Themes Control" on page 74.

Promote and Demote Headings

 Enter text in the Outline or click in an existing line of text to select it.

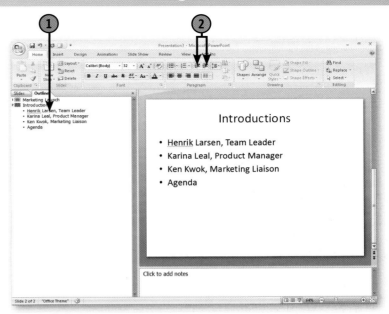

Click the Home tab and choose Decrease List Level or Increase List Level from the Paragraph group. Decrease demotes the heading; Increase promotes it to a higher level in the outline.

Tip

You can create many levels of indented bullets in an outline, but a couple of levels is usually the most you should ever have. As a rule, if you have that much detail to provide about a point, it really should be a separate slide. Also, in the typical presentation environment, attendees can't possibly see more than two levels of headings on the screen.

Tip

After you demote a heading to the bullet point level, when you press Enter to create the next heading it will also be at the bullet point level. When you're ready to start the next slide, you can type a heading and then promote it to slide title level. You can also use a shortcut to do this: press Shift+Tab to promote and Tab to demote a heading.

Try This!

In PowerPoint 2007, when you select text a Mini toolbar containing the most commonly used text formatting tools appears. You can use the Promote and Demote tool buttons on the Mini toolbar to structure your outline.

Working with Outline Contents

Once you have entered contents into your outline and demoted and promoted headings to create an outline structure, you may want to work with the outline contents in various ways. For example, you might want to view just the slide titles at times; at other times you will want to see all the detailed headings. You may also want to move headings around in an outline to reorganize the content.

Finally, text formatting is shown by default in an outline, but you can turn it off and back on easily, which can come in handy as you edit and review your slides.

Expand and Collapse the Outline

1. Click the Outline tab to display it, and right-click on a slide.

2. Do either of the following to collapse the outline:

   - Choose Collapse to hide all the subheads for this slide title.

   - Choose Collapse All to hide all the subheads for the presentation.

(continued on the next page)

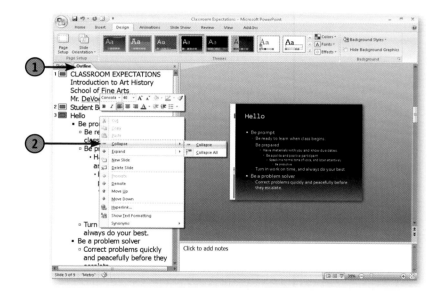

Expand and Collapse
the Outline *(continued)*

③ Do either of the following to
expand the outline:

- Choose Expand to display all
the subheads for this slide title.

- Choose Expand All to display all
subheads in the presentation.

Try This!

In a longer presentation, collapse
headings that you've finished working on to speed up scrolling through
your outline to find information you
need. When you are ready to view
all your contents again, right-click in
the Outline tab and choose Expand,
Expand All.

Tip

Collapsing or expanding your outline
will have no effect on what appears
in the Slide pane nor on what appears
when you give your slide presentation. A collapsed outline will still show
all headings at every level when you
give your presentation.

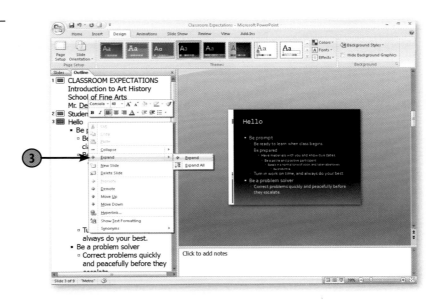

Move Slides or Text Up and Down in an Outline

(1) Right-click the line of text or right-click and drag to select multiple lines of text, that you want to move.

(2) Choose Move Up or Move Down from the shortcut menu. The selected line or lines move one line up or down together.

(3) To move the entire slide, you can click and drag the slide icon and drop it in a new position in the outline. A line appears indicating the new position of the text as you drag.

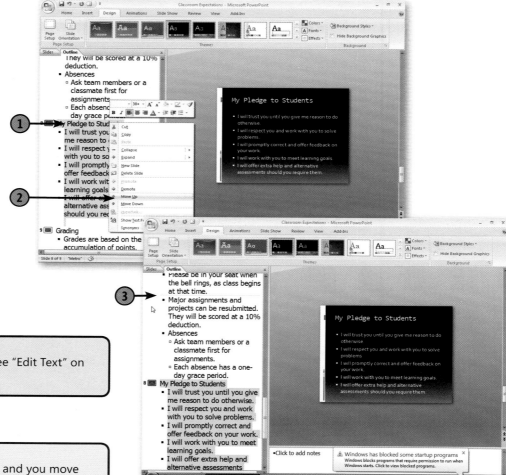

See Also

For information about editing text in slides, see "Edit Text" on page 43.

Tip

If slide subheads are collapsed under the title, and you move the title, all subheads move along with their slide title. If you don't want to move a subhead, you must first expand the slide and either move the subhead to another family of headings by cutting and pasting it elsewhere or promote it to be a slide title on its own.

Turn Formatting On and Off in an Outline

1. Right-click anywhere in the Outline tab.

2. Choose Show Text Formatting from the shortcut menu.

3. To return text to the way it was, right-click in the Outline pane and choose Show Text Formatting again.

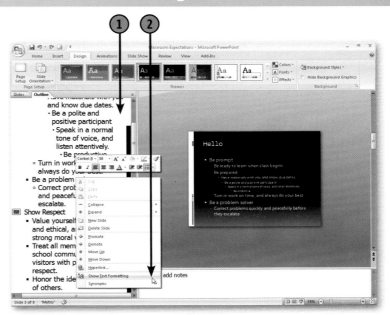

See Also

In PowerPoint 2007 there is no longer an Outline toolbar, so you choose most commands from the shortcut menu that appears when you right-click the outline. However, if you often use outline tools, consider placing a couple on the Quick Access Toolbar. For more information about how to do this, see "Customize the Quick Access Toolbar" on page 14

Tip

Showing formatting in the outline is a good way to see whether you have a good balance of fonts or formats such as bold in your presentation and to confirm that you have kept text formatting consistent overall. Another good way to view this is to display the Slide Sorter view.

Send an Outline to Word

① With the presentation open that you want to send, click the Office button.

② Click Publish.

③ Choose Create Handouts In Microsoft Office Word.

(continued on the next page)

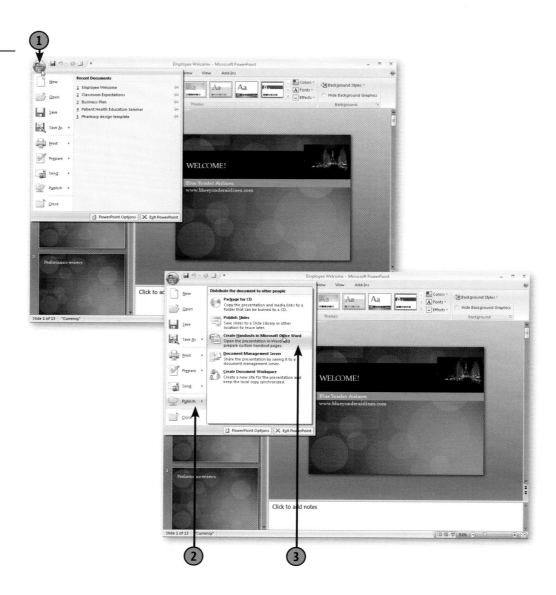

Send an Outline to Word *(continued)*

④ In the Send To Microsoft Office Word dialog box that appears, click the Outline Only option.

⑤ Click OK. Word opens with the outline displayed.

Tip

You can also print just the outline from PowerPoint by opening the Print dialog box (click the Office button and click Print) and choosing Outline View from the Print What drop-down list.

Try This!

If you work in the outline frequently, you may want to add the Outline View button to the Quick Access toolbar. This allows you to display just your outline, with no other panes to distract you.

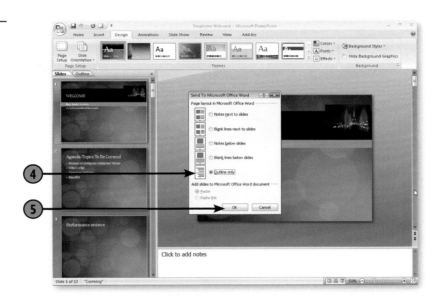

6 Managing and Viewing Slides

In this section:

- Viewing Slides in Slide Pane
- Managing Slides in Slide Sorter View
- Hiding Slides and Slide Elements

Once you have created some slides, you are likely to want to work with them to refine your content. For example, you may want to move among your slides to review their content, delete or copy certain slides, move slides, or hide them in the presentation.

The Slides tab is useful for viewing the slides in your presentation as thumbnails, which appear next to the larger view of the selected slide displayed in Normal view.

Sometimes while refining a presentation you will want to delete a slide that's no longer relevant or copy and paste a slide from one place or one presentation to another. There is also a handy, one step feature to duplicate a slide by copying and pasting. Sometimes the contents of your presentation need reorganizing, and when that happens, you can move slides around quite easily in Slide Sorter view.

Finally, you can choose not to show certain slides while running your presentation by hiding them. You can easily unhide them when you need to use them again. This makes it easy to customize presentations for different audiences.

Viewing Slides in Slide Pane

PowerPoint offers several views of your slides. In Normal view, the Slide pane is the central display of the currently selected slide. This is where you typically focus on the design elements of each slide. In addition, the Slides tab, which is coupled with the Outline tab to the left of the Slide pane, shows all the slides in your presentation in order. Use this tab to get an overview of the look and contents of all slides side by side with one slide shown in more detail.

Display Slides

1. Click the Slides tab in the Slides/Outline pane in Normal view; the Slides tab appears.

2. From the Slides tab do any of the following to move around your presentation:

   ■ Click the Scroll Down button to move ahead in the presentation.

   ■ Click the Scroll Up button to move back in the presentation.

   ■ Click and drag the scrollbar to move ahead or back in the presentation by one or more slides at a time.

3. Click a slide to select it; the slide is then displayed in the Slide pane.

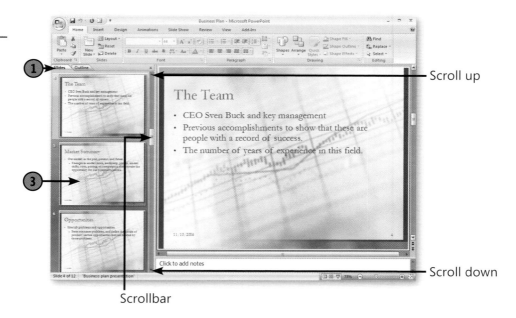
Scroll up
Scrollbar
Scroll down

Tip ✓

Can't find the Slides tab? If the Slides/Outline pane is not visible in Normal view, at some point you closed it. Just click the Normal view button to restore it.

Managing Slides in Slide Sorter View

As with anything you write, part of the process of building a PowerPoint presentation is revising and refining it as you go along. Just as you edit a report by deleting or copying a sentence, in a PowerPoint presentation you might delete a slide or copy it so you can base a new slide on existing contents.

It's also typical to rearrange the flow of your thoughts as you write. In PowerPoint that's as easy as moving a slide around in your presentation. All of these tasks are simple to do in the Slide Sorter view.

Delete Slides

① Click the Slide Sorter button to display Slide Sorter view.

② Right-click a slide.

③ Choose Delete Slide from the shortcut menu.

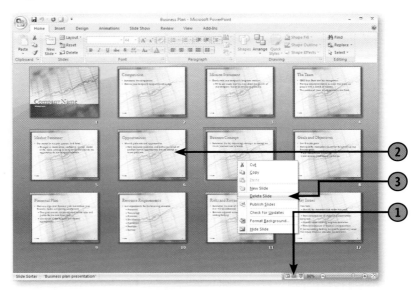

Caution !

If you delete a slide and save changes to your presentation, that slide is gone forever. Be sure you don't need any of a slide's contents before you delete it.

See Also

Instead of deleting a slide, you can temporarily hide it from view. Then if you decide you need the contents later, you can simply unhide it. See "Hiding and Unhiding Slides" later in this section for help with this feature.

Copy and Paste Slides

1. With Slide Sorter view displayed, click a slide.

2. Click the Home tab on the ribbon.

3. Click the Copy button.

4. Click the slide you want to paste the original slide after.

5. Click the Paste button on the Home tab.

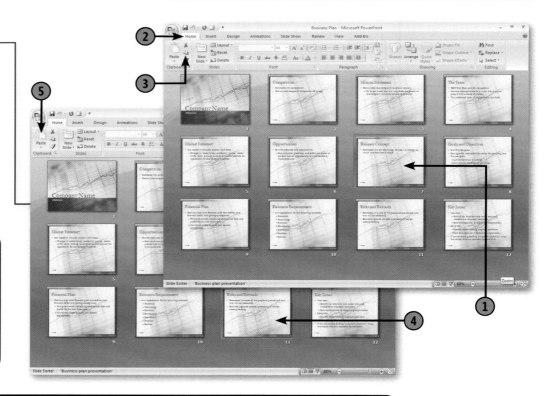

Tip ✓

You can also use keystroke shortcuts to cut and paste selected slides. Note that keystroke shortcuts are displayed in the super tooltips that appear when you hold your mouse over an item on the ribbon. Use Ctrl+X to cut, Ctrl+V to paste, and Ctrl+C to copy.

See Also

Use the procedures here to cut, copy, and paste whole slides. For more about cutting, copying, and pasting specific elements from the contents of slides, see "Cut, Copy, and Paste Text" on page 45.

Duplicate Slides

1. With Slide Sorter view displayed, click a slide.

2. Click the Home tab on the ribbon.

3. Click the arrow on the New Slide button and choose Duplicate Selected Slides. The duplicate slide appears to the right of the original slide.

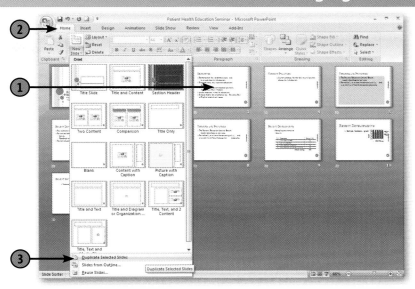

Tip

After you duplicate a slide, you can move the duplicate wherever you like in the presentation and make changes to it. See the next task for more about moving slides.

Tip

You can also cut, copy, paste, and duplicate slides by using the Slides tab in Normal view. Just right-click on any slide in the tab and choose the appropriate command from the shortcut menu that appears.

Move a Slide

1 With Slide Sorter view displayed, click on a slide.

2 Drag the slide and drop it where you want it to appear. A vertical line indicates the new position.

3 Release your mouse button to drop the slide where you want it in the presentation.

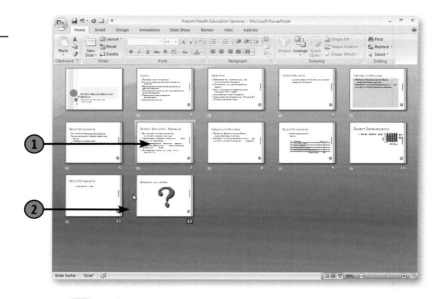

Tip

You can use the Outline tab in Normal view to move slides around in text form. Right-click a slide icon and choose Move Up or Move Down to move a slide one position at a time, or drag the icon and drop it in any other position in the outline.

See Also

For more about managing slides in the Outline tab, see "Move Slides or Text Up and Down in an Outline: on page 60.

Hiding Slides and Slide Elements

There may be times when you want to use a subset of slides for a presentation, or perhaps need to hide a single slide because it contains information not appropriate to a particular audience. For example, you may choose not to show a management benefits slide when making a presentation about benefits to non-managers. In that case, you can easily hide the slide, give the presentation, and then unhide it.

Hide and Unhide Slides

(1) Click the Slide Sorter view button.

(2) Click a slide to select it. If you wish to hide more than one slide, hold down Ctrl and click additional slides to select them.

(3) Click the Slide Show tab on the ribbon.

(4) Click the Hide Slide button in the Setup group to hide all selected slides.

- A gray box appears over the slide number indicating it is hidden and will not appear when you run the presentation.

(5) With the Slide Sorter view displayed, click the slide or slides you want to unhide.

(6) In the Slide Show tab, click the Hide Slide button in the Setup group. The gray box disappears from around the slide number. The slide will now appear when you run the presentation.

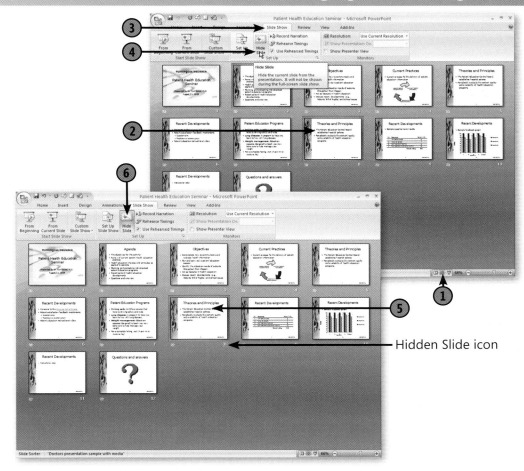

Hidden Slide icon

Try This!

Try printing a presentation that includes hidden slides. When you display the Print dialog box, you can click the Print Hidden Slides checkbox in the Print dialog box so slides you've hidden will be included in the print out.

See Also

For more information about printing presentations with hidden slides, see "Choose Which Slides to Print" on page 206.

Using Slide Layouts and Themes

In this section:

- **Understanding What Slide Layouts and Themes Control**
- **Working with Layouts**
- **Working with Themes**
- **Changing Theme Colors and Fonts**

A presentation has to have solid content and clearly fleshed out topics, but in addition, it must hold your audience's attention. Visual enhancements such as color, font styles, and graphics go a long way toward impressing your audience with your professional approach.

Microsoft has built in several design aspects for your presentations in PowerPoint 2007. These design elements, including themes, color schemes, and slide layouts, offer a built-in consistency through a common look and feel. This design consistency means that you don't have to be a graphic designer to design an attractive presentation.

Themes can be applied to individual slides or multiple slides in your presentation. A theme includes background colors, graphics, font styles and sizes, and alignment of placeholders and text.

Layouts control how many and what types of placeholders appear on a slide. For example, a layout may contain only a slide title placeholder, or a slide title plus content (content placeholders can contain several kinds of content, such as a chart, table, picture, SmartArt object, or movie).

Color schemes are preset combinations of colors for your slide backgrounds, text, and graphic elements.

What Slide Layouts and Themes Control

Slide layouts provide a basic structure to your slides by including placeholders that may contain title or subtitle text, bulleted lists, or a variety of graphic elements (referred to as "content"), and captions in a variety of combinations. By selecting the right slide layout, you make the job of adding text and content easier, as placeholders can help to automate the building of slides.

Slide layout gallery

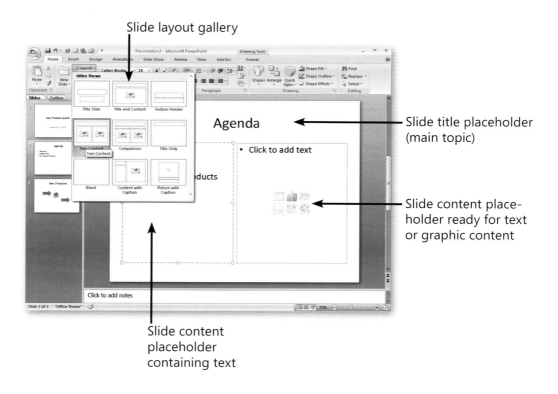

Slide title placeholder (main topic)

Slide content placeholder ready for text or graphic content

Slide content placeholder containing text

While slide layouts control the types of slide content, slide themes are concerned with the design elements of a slide. These may include a background color or effect such as a gradient; font styles, sizes, and alignment; bullet styles; and graphic elements.

Background colors

Theme gallery

Font

Graphic element

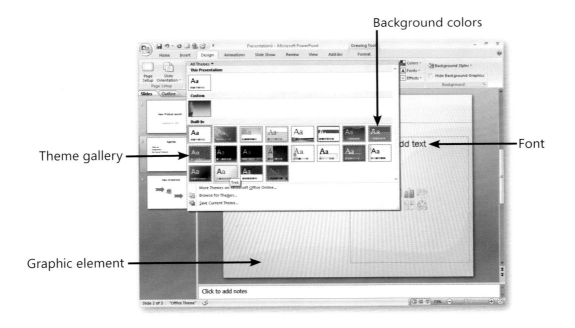

Working with Layouts

A slide layout in PowerPoint is like a blueprint for a house; it establishes the various types of "rooms" that appear on your slide. Just as certain types of rooms contain certain types of furniture, slides can contain different types of objects. A title and content slide will hold a title and bullet list, while a picture with caption layout will hold an image and some text describing it. The placeholders in a layout automate tasks involved with creating and formatting contents specific to each type placeholder.

Apply a Layout

(1) Display the slide whose layout you want to change and click the Home tab.

(2) Click the Layout button to open the Layout gallery.

(3) Click a layout to apply it.

(continued on the next page)

Try This!

You can determine a slide's layout when you first create it. Click the Home tab and click the arrow on the New Slide button. Click on the layout you prefer, and the slide is created with that layout applied.

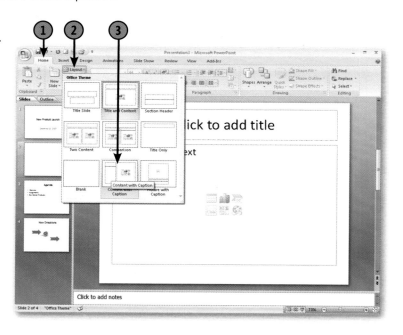

Apply a Layout *(continued)*

④ The placeholders specified by that layout appear.

Tip

In PowerPoint 2003 and earlier versions, there were slide lay-outs with bullet point content and others with graphic and multimedia content. In PowerPoint 2007, layouts with content now include both bullet point and graphic/multimedia content tools on one slide. You have to pick one or the other, though: When you use either of these tools to add content to these placeholders, the other tool disappears.

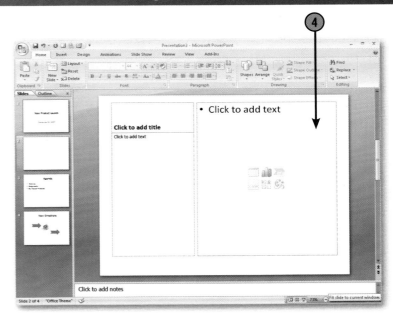

Add a Placeholder to a Slide Layout

1. Click the View tab.

2. Click the Slide Master button. The Slide Master appears.

3. Click the Insert Placeholder button.

4. Select a style of placeholder to insert.

(continued on the next page)

Tip

If you'd rather create an additional placeholder on one slide only, try duplicating an existing placeholder. Select a placeholder on the slide and, on the Home tab, click the arrow on the Paste button and choose the Duplicate command. A copy of the placeholder is pasted on the slide.

Add a Placeholder to a
Slide Layout (continued)

⑤ Click and drag to draw the placeholder where you want it to appear on the slide.

⑥ If necessary, click on the placeholder to select it and drag it to a new position on the slide.

⑦ Click the Close Master View button to close the Slide Master. The additional placeholder will appear on every slide of that type in the presentation.

See Also

For information about displaying the Slide Master view, see "Display and Navigate Masters" on page 145.

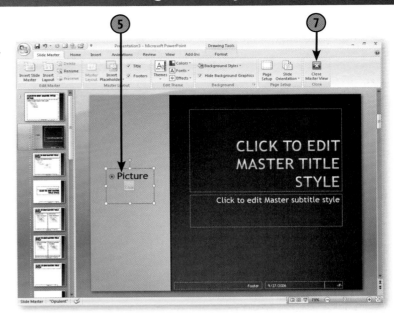

Working with Themes

Themes in PowerPoint provide a suite of design settings that give your slides a consistent look and feel. You can apply a theme with a single action, putting in place background graphics and colors, font and font size settings, and a layout. The gallery of themes located on the Design tab helps you preview and choose the best look for your presentation easily.

Tip

You can find additional themes online. Because nearly everybody who creates PowerPoint presentations picks from the same set of built-in themes, at some point you may want to show folks something entirely new. Finding updated themes becomes a way to differentiate your presentation.

See Also

For information about making individual changes to design elements on slides, see Section 9.

Apply a Slide Theme

1. Click the Design tab.

2. Click the More arrow on the Themes gallery.

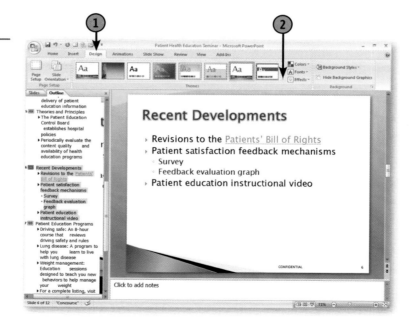

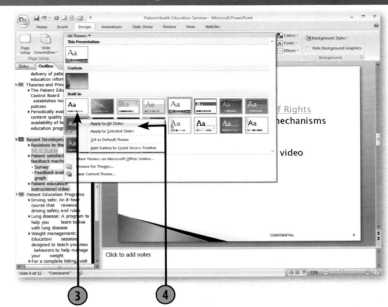

3 Move your mouse cursor over the themes to preview them on your slides.

4 Right-click a theme and click one of two options:

- Choose Apply To All Slides to apply the theme to every slide in your presentation.

- Choose Apply To Selected Slides to apply the theme only to the currently selected slide or slides.

When you apply a new theme, it creates a master. For more information about working with slide masters, see "Understanding How Slide Master Works" on page 144 .

Tip ✔

If you want to apply a theme to several slides, it's easiest to display the Slide Sorter view, click the first slide you want to apply the theme to, and then hold down the Ctrl key and click other slides. Then follow the preceding steps to apply the theme to multiple selected slides.

Find Slide Themes Online

1. With your computer logged onto the Internet, click the Design tab.

2. Click the More arrow on the Theme gallery.

3. Choose More Themes On Microsoft Office Online.

4. In the Office Online Web site, enter a search term to search for a template.

5. Click Search.

6. In the results that appear, click on a thumbnail.

(continued on the next page)

Tip

By default, the blank Office theme is applied to new presentations. You can set a different theme as the default theme to be applied to every new presentation. First locate the theme in the Theme gallery and then right-click it and select Set As Default Theme.

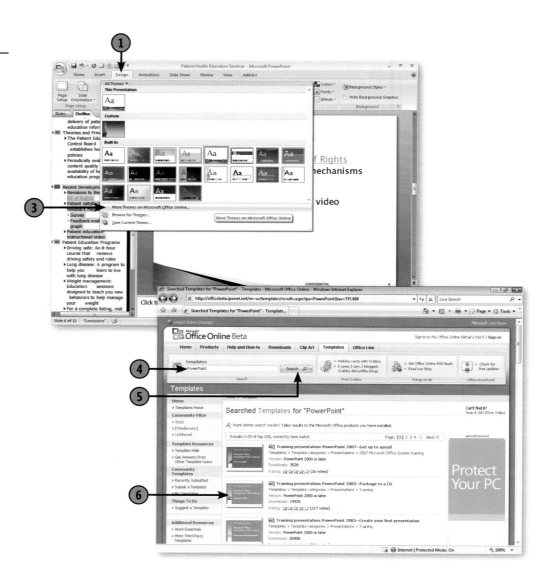

⑦ Click the Download Now button to download the template. PowerPoint will automatically open a new presentation with your new template applied.

Tip

If you can't find a theme you thought you had downloaded, try choosing the Browse For Themes command at the bottom of the Theme gallery. In the Choose Theme or Themed Document dialog box that opens, enter the name of the theme (the Office Themes and Themed Document format is specified by default) or use tools to browse for the theme in the various folders on your computer.

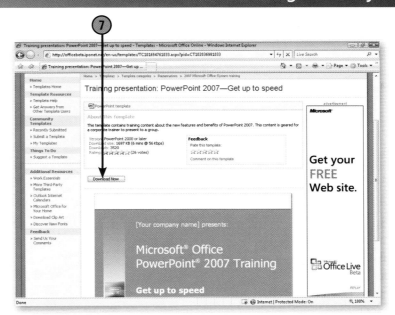

Changing Theme Colors and Fonts

Themes include settings for colors and fonts. A theme's color scheme affects most elements on your slide, including background, text, and graphics. Themes provide sets of colors that work well together so your slides should maintain an attractive and cohesive look no matter which one you apply. Font schemes include settings for heading and body fonts. When you apply a theme, it contains a preset color scheme and fonts, but you can change these to give your slides a new look.

Select a Different Theme Color Scheme

① Click the Design tab.

② Click the Colors button in the Themes group.

③ Right-click on a color scheme and choose either Apply To All Slides or Apply To Selected Slides. The new colors are applied.

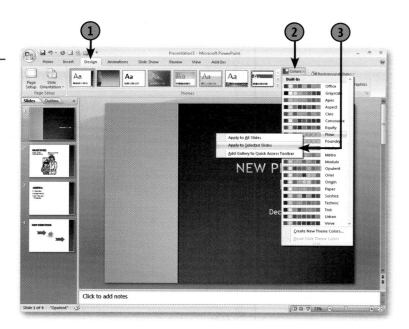

Tip

Be sure to use color combinations that work well in the space where you will give your presentation. Most color combinations PowerPoint offers should help to keep your text readable, but if you decide to change the color of an individual element yourself, remember that dark text colors are hard to read in a lighter space.

See Also

You can also apply theme elements to all slides by applying them through the Slide Master. For more information about working with masters, see "Display and Navigate Masters" on page 145..

Change Theme Fonts

① Click the Design tab.

② Click the Fonts button.

③ Move your mouse over the fonts to preview them on your slides.

④ Click a font style to apply it to all slides.

Try This!

To create your own font theme, choose Create New Theme Fonts from the Fonts gallery. Select a heading font and body font, give the font theme a name, and click Save. The theme is now available in the Fonts gallery.

See Also

To learn how to manually change fonts on selected text, see "Applying Fonts" on page 124.

8

Inserting and Drawing Objects

In this section:

- Working with Tables
- Creating and Modifying Charts
- Inserting Clip Art
- Creating WordArt
- Working with SmartArt
- Working with Pictures
- Inserting Media Objects
- Creating a Photo Album
- Drawing Shapes and Text Boxes

The ability to add graphic elements to your slides allows you to add visual pizzazz to your presentation that helps keep viewers entertained and interested. In a multimedia-savvy world, people expect more than black bullet points and a white background, and PowerPoint helps you meet those expectations.

Although visual elements should never overpower the contents of your presentation, some visual elements such as photographs or charts might actually help you convey your message in a "picture is worth a thousand words" way. Sometimes you will use elements such as illustrations, shapes, or WordArt effects simply to add visual interest.

In this section you explore the process of inserting various visual elements into slides, such as tables, charts, pictures, Clip Art, WordArt, sounds, and even movie clips. Once you've inserted such elements, move on to Section 9 where you discover how to format and modify those elements to best effect.

Creating Tables

Tables offer a way to present information in a way that suggests the relationships among various sets of data using the visual elements of separate cells organized by rows and columns.

Tables also offer the option of formatting those columns and rows with color and shading, which helps the person viewing the table to differentiate among sets of data at a glance.

Insert a Table

1. Click the Insert tab.

2. Click the Table button.

3. In the Insert Table drop down, click and drag across the squares to select the number of rows and columns you want to include in your table.

(continued on the next page)

Try This!

You can also insert a table using the icons that appear in any empty content placeholder. Click the upper left icon in the set of icons that appears in these placeholders to display a dialog box where you can specify the number of rows and columns for the table.

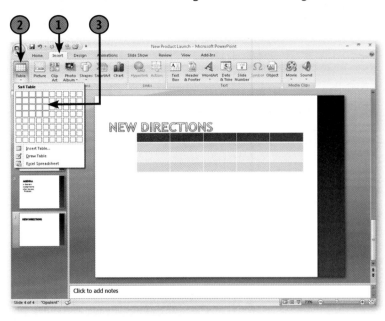

Insert a Table (continued)

④ When you release your mouse, the table appears on your slide.

⑤ The Table Tools Design tab is displayed.

See Also

Although this section deals with the basics of inserting tables, please see "Edit Tables" on page 92 for more about formatting tables.

Try This!

The Comparison slide layout includes a title placeholder, two subtitle place-holders, and two content placehold-ers. If you want to include two tables that viewers can compare side by side with a heading to describe the con-tents of each, this is a useful layout to use.

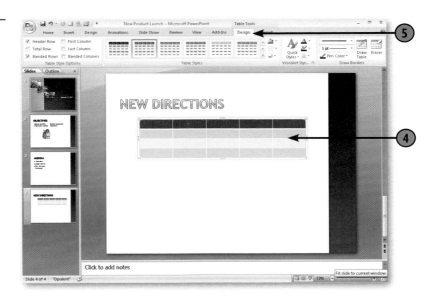

Insert Rows and Columns

1 Click the table to select it.

2 Click the Table Tools, Layout tab.

Tip

You can split the cells of a column in two in your table to include two sets of data without having to add a new column. Select the column as described in Step 3 on the next page and on the Table Tools, Layout tab click the Split Cells button. In the Split Cells dialog box, click OK to accept the default number of columns. The column splits in two parts, and you can enter text in each.

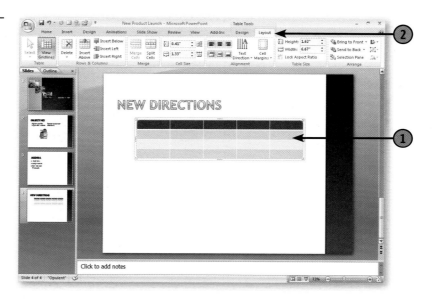

Insert Rows and Columns *(continued)*

(3) Hold your mouse above a column or to the left of a row until the cursor becomes an arrow and click to select the column or row.

(4) Click the Insert Left or Insert Right button to insert a column to the left or right of the selected column.

(5) Click the Insert Above or Insert Below button to insert a row above or below the selected row.

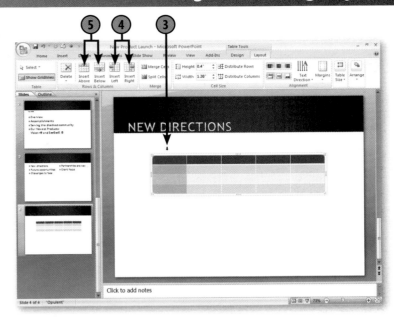

Editing Tables

There are several things you can do to help make your tables more easily readable, including adding borders to cells to keep the information separate, aligning text in cells both horizontally and vertically, and merging cells so that, for example, the title of a table can run across all the columns in the table.

Modify Table Borders

1. Click and drag across a table to select all its cells.
2. Click the Table Tools, Design tab.
3. Click the Border tool.

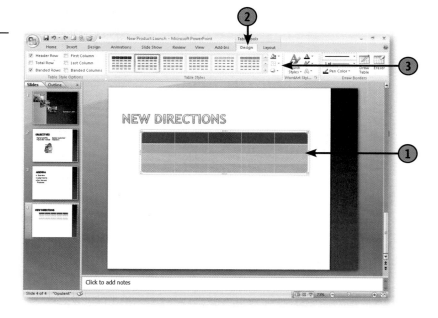

Modify Table Borders *(continued)*

④ Choose a border style such as All Borders to outline each and every cell in the table or Outside Borders to surround the outside of the table with a border.

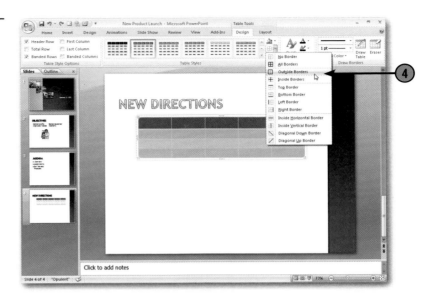

Try This!

You can use the Draw Table tool to draw borders around cells one by one. Click the Draw Table tool on the Table Tools, Design tab, and then, using the pencil-shaped mouse cursor, click on any cell edge to draw a line. This method draws only one cell edge at a time. To get rid of any cell border, you can use the Erase tool on the same tab.

See Also

For information about formatting table styles and adding background colors, see "Formatting Objects" on page 130.

Align Text in Cells

1 Click and drag across the cells to select the ones whose text you want to align.

2 Click the Table Tools, Layout tab.

3 Click the Align Left, Center, or Align Right buttons to align the text from left to right in the cells.

4 Click the Align Top, Center Vertically, or Align Bottom buttons to align the text between the top of the cells and the bottom of the cells.

You can also click the Arrange button on the Home tab, click Align, and then choose any of the alignment commands from a drop down menu that appears.

To align a table relative to the edges of your slides, click Arrange, Align, and choose Align To Slide.

Merge Cells

1. Click and drag to select the cells you want to merge.

2. Click the Table Tools, Layout tab.

3. Click the Merge Cells button. The selected cells are merged into one.

Try This!

To return the merged cells to individual cells again, click and drag to select the cell, and then on the Table Tools, Layout tab click the Split Cells button. In the dialog box that appears, enter the number of columns or rows you want to split the merged cell into and click OK. The merged cell is split into the number of individual cells you indicated.

Tip

You can merge any number of cells including cells in multiple rows and columns. This is often useful for tables you use to create forms that may have nonuniform cells for holding different types of information or pictures of various sizes.

Creating Charts

Charts in PowerPoint are based on Excel's charting feature. When you insert a chart, Excel opens for you to enter the underlying data for the chart. When Excel opens, it holds some sample data, which should help you in entering your specific data in the proper format to form the basis of a chart. Charts are wonderful tools for providing lots of information in a quickly understood, visual format. PowerPoint's chart feature offers dozens of styles of charts to choose from.

Insert a Chart

1. Click the Insert tab.
2. Click the Chart button.
3. Click a category of chart type on the left.
4. Click a chart style from the thumbnails displayed.
5. Click OK.

(continued on the next page)

Try This!

You can also insert a chart using the icons that appear in any empty content placeholder. Click the icon in the middle of the top row of icons that appears in these placeholders to display the Create Chart dialog box, where you can specify the type and style of chart as outlined in the previous steps.

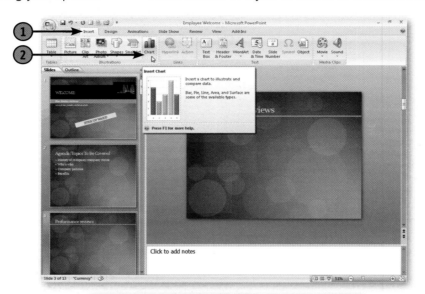

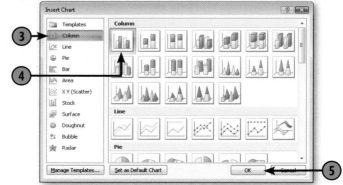

Insert a Chart *(continued)*

⑥ Modify the sample data with your own source data for the chart.

⑦ Click the Close button in the Excel window to return to PowerPoint and view the chart.

⑧ The chart appears on your Power-Point slide.

Tip

You can change the chart type at any time by clicking Change Chart Type under the Chart Tools, Design tab. The Change Chart Type dialog box (which is identical to the Create Chart dialog box) appears for you to select another type of chart.

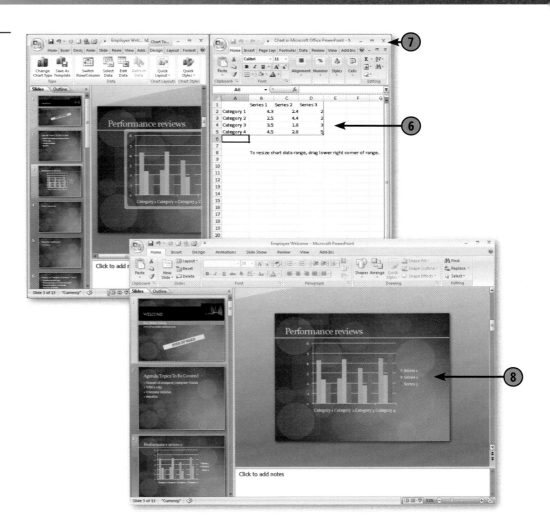

Change Chart Style and Layout

① Click a chart to select it.

② Click the Chart Tools, Design tab.

③ Click the More button on the Chart Layouts gallery.

④ Click a new layout to apply it.

⑤ Click the More button on the Chart Styles gallery.

(continued on the next page)

Tip

Chart Types control the chart objects, such as whether your chart uses bars, lines, or pie wedges to represent data. Chart Layouts control whether your chart includes a legend, the source data, and elements such as grid lines. The Chart Styles gallery offers sets of colors for chart elements and the chart background.

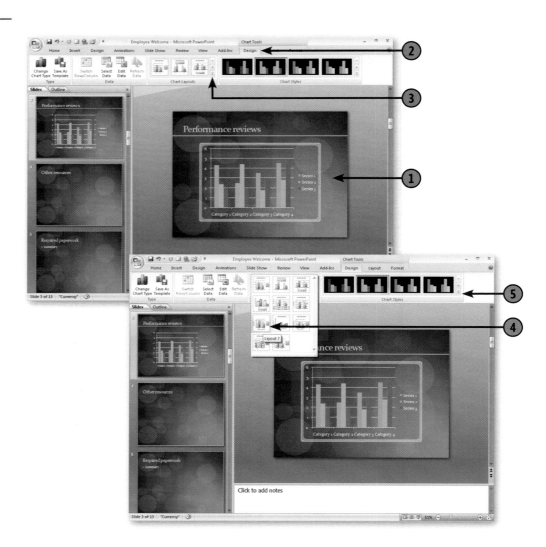

Change Chart Style and
Layout *(continued)*

6 Click a new style to apply it.

Tip

A layout applies formatting to your chart, but you can modify each aspect of the chart layout manually using the tools on the Chart Tools, Layout tab. The next procedure explains how to modify the legend display, for example.

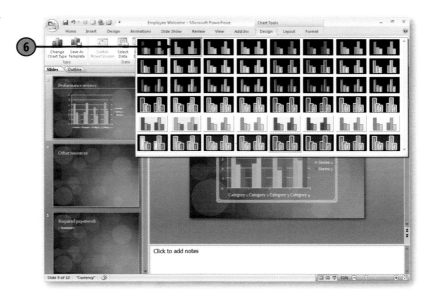

Display or Hide a Chart Legend

① Click on a chart to select it.

② Click the Chart Tools, Layout tab.

③ Click the Legend button.

(continued on the next page)

Tip

Rather than choosing a placement for the legend by selecting a layout or using the Legend button, you can move the legend to any position you want by clicking and dragging it within the chart box.

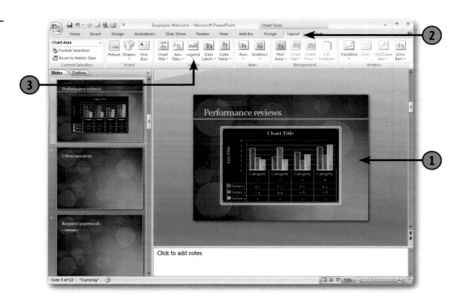

Display or Hide a Chart Legend *(continued)*

④ Click a layout position for the legend, or, to turn the legend off, click None.

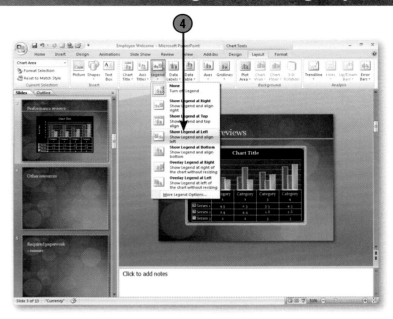

Try This!

You can format a legend by right-clicking it in the chart and choosing Format Legend. In the Format Legend dialog box that appears, you can modify the position of the legend and the line style surrounding it, add a fill color as a background for it, and so on.

Adding Clip Art

Clip art is a treasure trove of absolutely free art you can use in your presentations to help get your message across or simply to add some visual excitement. Clip art includes photos, illustrations, movies, and sounds. When you installed PowerPoint, it came with one collection of clip art; however, you can also browse the Internet to access other collections. You can use the Clip Art task pane to search for and insert clip art.

See Also

For information about rotating clip art objects, see "Rotating and Flipping Objects" on page 135.

Caution

Although clip art is typically free, other art you find on the Internet is not. You must get permission to use any art or text you find online and sometimes must pay a fee. If you want additional free clip art, a safe bet is to go to Microsoft Office's Web site and browse for clip art collections.

Search for Clip Art

(1) With a layout containing a content placeholder displayed, click the Clip Art icon.

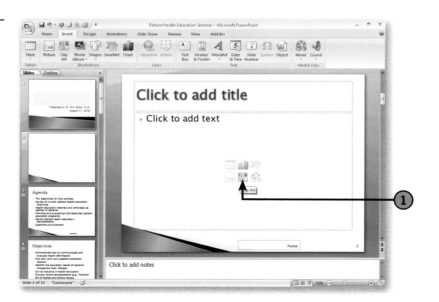

Search for Clip Art *(continued)*

② Enter a search term in the Search For text box to find related art.

③ Click the arrow on the Search In field and choose the collections to search.

④ Click the arrow on the Results Should Be field and choose the format of media you want to search.

⑤ Click Go.

Tip

To view clip art collections available from Microsoft's Office Web site, you can click the Clip Art On Office Online link at the bottom of the Clip Art task pane. You must be logged on to the Internet for this to work.

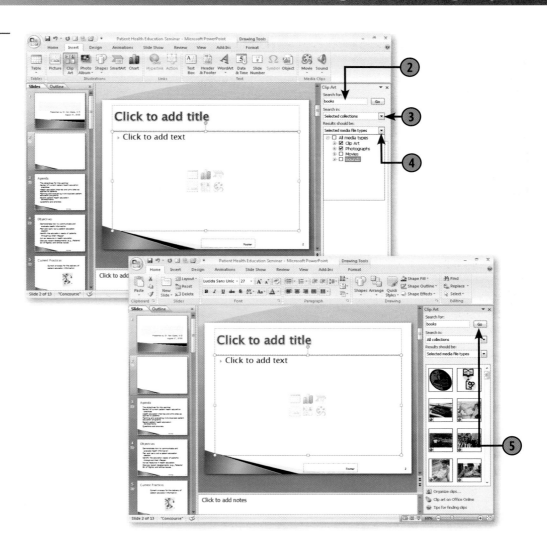

Insert Clip Art

1 After performing a search for clip art, in the Clip Art task pane scroll through the results using the scrollbar.

2 To insert a clip click the thumbnail of the clip, or...

3 Click the arrow along the side of the clip and choose Insert.

(continued on the next page)

Tip

After you locate a clip you want to use, you can also drag and drop it onto a slide in your presentation.

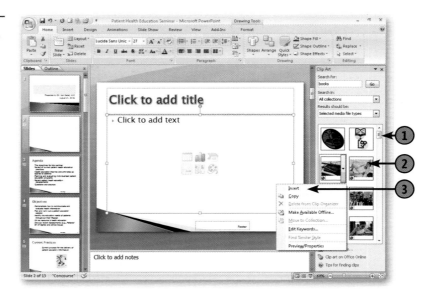

Insert Clip Art *(continued)*

④ The clip art will be inserted in your placeholder.

Try This!

You don't have to use a content placeholder to insert clip art; you can insert it anywhere on any slide layout by clicking the Clip Art button on the Insert tab. This opens the Clip Art task pane. Follow the steps in the Search for Clip Art task to locate and insert clip art on your slide.

Tip

Clip art often appears larger than you may want it for your presentation, overlapping other elements on your slide. Don't worry! Section 9 provides steps for resizing and moving clip art on your slides.

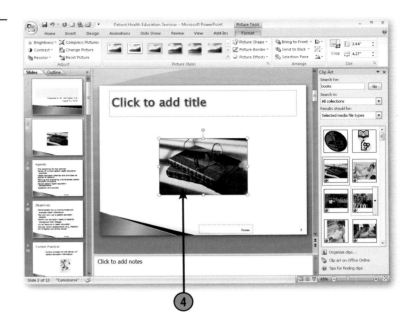

Creating WordArt

WordArt is a tool that allows you to apply interesting effects such as curves or 3-D effects to any text. WordArt is best used to call attention to an important, short phrase, such as "Free!" or "All New," because the distortions of WordArt designs can make longer phrases hard to read. You first insert a WordArt placeholder, enter text into it, and then apply various effects to it.

Insert WordArt

① Click the Insert tab.

② Click the WordArt button.

③ Click a WordArt style.

④ Type your text in the placeholder.

(continued on the next page)

Try This!

You can also select typed text in your presentation and then follow the steps to insert WordArt. In that case, the WordArt placeholder appears with the selected text already displayed in it.

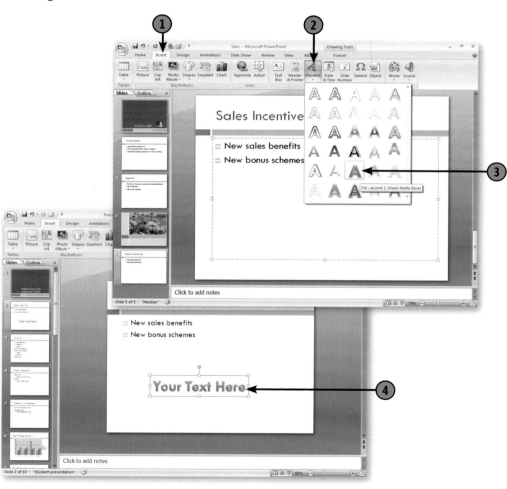

Insert WordArt *(continued)*

5 Click outside the placeholder to view the WordArt.

Tip

You can resize WordArt easily by clicking on a handle around the edges and dragging out or in. To keep the object's original proportions, be sure to drag on a corner handle only.

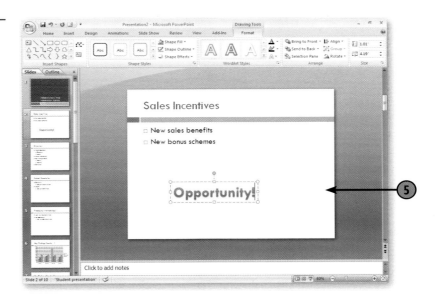

Apply Effects to WordArt

① Click the WordArt object to select it.

② Click the Drawing Tools, Format tab.

③ Click the Shape Effects button.

(continued on the next page)

Tip

In previous versions of PowerPoint, you chose one set of effects such as shape, 3-D perspective, and colors to apply to your WordArt. In PowerPoint 2007, WordArt offers more powerful design tools, although you have to apply various effects individually. You can use the Shape Effects, Shape Outline, and Shape Fill tools on the Drawing Tools, Format tab to individually apply these effects. You can also use the QuickStyles gallery to choose preset combinations of effects.

Apply Effects to WordArt *(continued)*

④ Move your mouse over a category and another drop-down gallery appears.

⑤ Move your mouse over various effects, and they are pre-viewed on your WordArt object.

⑥ Click an effect, and it's applied to the WordArt. You can apply multiple categories of effects.

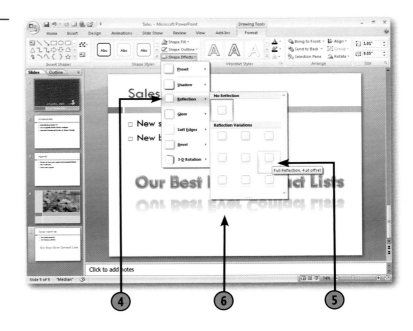

Working with SmartArt

A new feature in PowerPoint 2007 is SmartArt, a souped-up diagramming tool that allows you to quickly create all kinds of diagrams and workflow charts. When you select and insert a SmartArt diagram, you can then use a simple outline pane to enter the text that populates the various boxes and shapes of the diagram. You can insert or delete elements easily. SmartArt also works like the shapes built into PowerPoint, so after you insert a diagram, you can change various elements of it by altering their shapes, adding shapes, modifying their colors, and more.

Insert SmartArt

① Display a slide with a layout containing a content placeholder.

② Click the SmartArt icon in the placeholder.

③ In the Choose a SmartArt Graphic dialog box that appears, click on a category on the left.

④ Click on a style on the right.

⑤ Click OK to insert the SmartArt object.

Tip

You can close the text entry box to the left of a SmartArt object by clicking the Close button in the top right corner. To redisplay it, click the left-facing arrow along the left side of the SmartArt object.

Tip

Some SmartArt styles include picture icons. Click on these to display the Insert Picture dialog box. Locate a picture file you want to use and click Insert. This is useful for diagrams such as organizational charts where you can insert photos of individuals in the organization.

See Also

For more information about working with objects on your slides, see "Formatting Objects" on page 130.

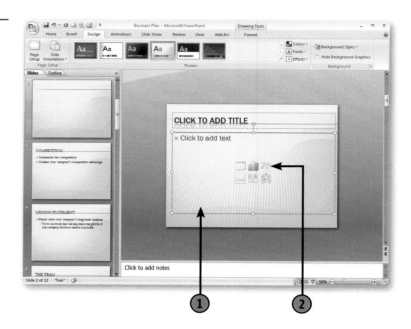

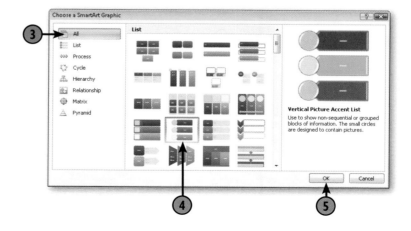

Add Text to SmartArt

① Click on the SmartArt placeholder to open it for editing.

② Type the first heading text.

③ Click in the next text box and type the next heading.

④ Headings appear in the SmartArt graphic. Press the up or down arrows on your keyboard to move between headings, and continue to fill in the headings. If you want to add an additional heading, press Enter after typing a heading and a new one will be created.

Tip

You don't have to use a content place-holder to insert SmartArt. Just click the Insert tab and click the SmartArt button to insert SmartArt on any slide.

Tip

Tab works a little differently in SmartArt. If you press Tab after clicking on a heading placeholder, your cursor does not move to the next heading as it does in some forms and programs. If you click on a heading placeholder and press Tab, it will indent one level. If you click on a heading and press Shift+Tab, it will move up one level in the outline.

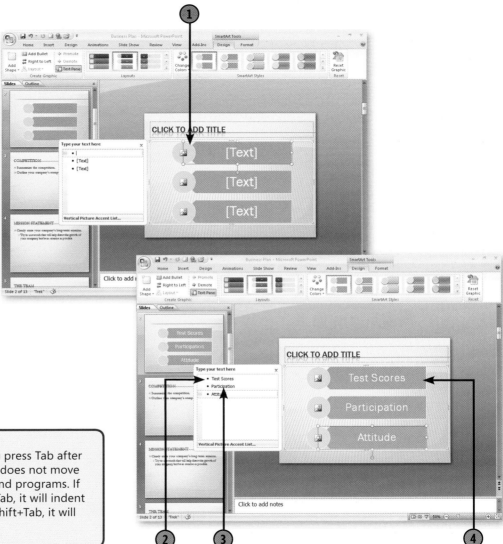

Working with Pictures

If you have taken photos yourself or somebody has provided photos, you will find that they can add to your presentation's impact. Perhaps you have a photo of your newest product for a sales presentation, or a photo of your soccer team in action for a school sports presentation. Inserting a photo onto a slide is easy to do. Once a picture is inserted, you can also crop it to trim out any unwanted portions using the Crop tool.

Insert a Picture

1 Display a slide with a layout that contains a content placeholder.

2 Click the Insert Picture From File icon.

3 Locate the picture file you want to insert.

4 Click the Open button.

(continued on the next page)

Insert a Picture *(continued)*

5 The picture appears on the slide.

See Also

The Photo Album feature is new to PowerPoint 2007. It allows you to create groups of photos to help you organize your images. For more about this feature, see "Creating a Photo Album" on page 118.

Tip

Insert a picture anywhere on a slide by clicking the Picture button on the Insert tab.

See Also

For more information about formatting pictures using the Picture Tools, Format tab of the ribbon, see "Working with Picture Tools" on page 138.

Crop a Picture

① Click a picture to select it.

② Click the Picture Tools, Format tab.

③ Click the Crop button.

(continued on the next page)

Tip

If you just want a smaller picture, rather than removing some of the picture by cropping, you can simply resize it. To resize a picture select it, and then click on any of the surrounding handles that appear and drag in or out.

Crop a Picture *(continued)*

④ Click on any line and drag inward to crop the picture. Continue cropping from various sides until the picture appears as you wish.

⑤ Press the Esc key or click any-where outside of the picture to turn off the cropping tool.

Tip

If you crop too much from your picture you can use the cropping tool to drag outward again, restoring the portion you cropped. You can even do this after deactivating the cropping session where you first trimmed the picture. As soon as you save the file, though, this cropping in reverse method will not work to restore your picture.

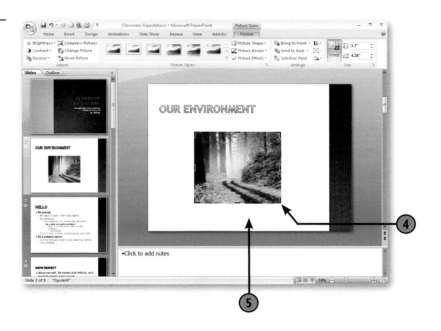

Working with Media Objects

Sprinkling sounds and animations in your presentations can add some sparkle or even help you bring a point home with flair. When you insert multimedia objects into slides, a movie object is indicated with an illustration icon, and a sound object is indicated with a small speaker icon. You can choose to have the animation or sound play as soon as the slide it is placed on appears, or when you click on the object while running in Slide Show view.

Insert a Movie or Sound

① Click the Insert tab.

② Click the Movie or Sound button.

(continued on the next page)

Tip

You can also choose to insert a media clip from the Clip Art task pane. When searching for clip art just select Movies or Sounds in the Results Should Be list. By inserting a media clip in this way, you can use a preview feature to see or hear it before inserting the object. See "Adding Clip Art" on page 102 for more about how to do this.

Insert a Movie or Sound *(continued)*

③ Locate the file you want to insert and click OK.

④ Click either Automatically or When Clicked to select how you want the object to run.

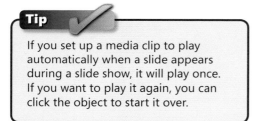

Tip

If you set up a media clip to play automatically when a slide appears during a slide show, it will play once. If you want to play it again, you can click the object to start it over.

Creating a Photo Album

If you want to create a slide show or a portion of a show that consists of a series of photos, you can use a new feature called Photo Album. A photo album is essentially a tool you use to set up a series of photos and text boxes, one each per slide in sequence. You can include captions for the photos if you wish, and you can also make use of some photo editing tools included in the Photo Album feature. These tools allow you to rotate the photos or change the brightness or contrast.

Insert a New Photo Album

① Click the Insert tab.

② Click the Photo Album button.

③ Click the File/Disk button.

④ Locate a picture to insert and then click the Insert button. Repeat this for as many photos as you wish to include in the album.

(continued on the next page)

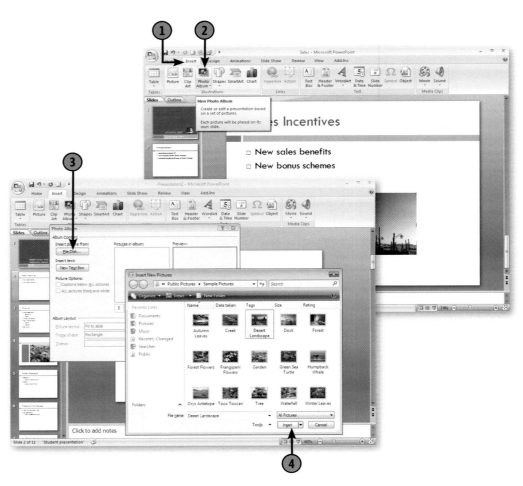

Insert a New Photo
Album *(continued)*

(5) If you want to include a text slide, click the New Text Box button.

(6) Use any of the tools to modify your photo album.

(7) Click Create to save the album. The new presentation is created. Save it as a standalone presentation or insert it into a larger presentation if you wish.

Try This!

You can edit a photo album once you've created it. Click the arrow on the Photo Album button and choose Edit Photo Album on the Insert tab. In the Edit Photo Album dialog box, you can use the tools to remove photos, add photos, rearrange photos, or change any of the picture or layout options.

See Also

After you create a photo album, you can modify the individual pictures by resizing, rotating, or moving them on the slides. For more information about working with objects, see "Rotating and Flipping Objects" on page 135.

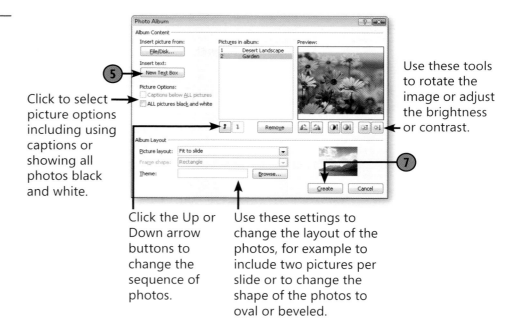

Click to select picture options including using captions or showing all photos black and white.

Use these tools to rotate the image or adjust the brightness or contrast.

Click the Up or Down arrow buttons to change the sequence of photos.

Use these settings to change the layout of the photos, for example to include two pictures per slide or to change the shape of the photos to oval or beveled.

Drawing Shapes and Text Boxes

You can use the Shapes feature of PowerPoint to draw a variety of objects, from lines, arrows, and boxes, to scrolls, callouts, and action buttons. When you draw a shape you can enter text in it; however that text will not appear in your presentation outline. If you draw an action button you can then associate an action, such as running another program or playing a sound that activates when you click the button during a slide show. In addition to various shapes, you can draw a text box, which is simply a placeholder where you can enter text; by default a text box has no border so the text appears to float on your page. Text in text boxes will not be reflected in the presentation outline.

Draw a Shape

1. Click the Insert tab.
2. Click the Shapes button.
3. Click on a shape. Your cursor changes to a plus symbol.
4. Click anywhere on your slide and drag to draw the object whatever size you need.

(continued on the next page)

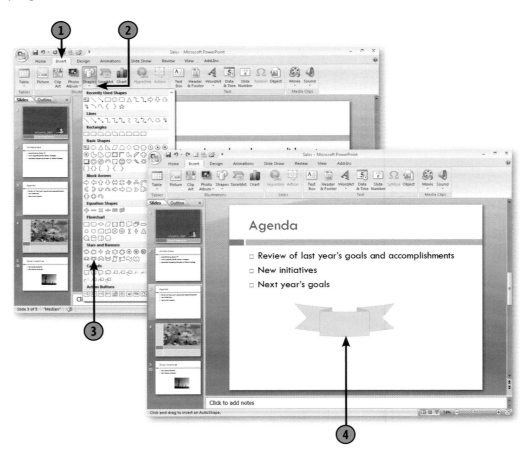

Draw a Shape *(continued)*

⑤ If you have drawn an action button, a dialog box appears where you can choose to go to another slide or presentation, run a program, run a macro, initiate an action, or play a sound. Establish the settings you need.

⑥ Click OK to save the settings.

Try This!

You can use an action button setting to link to a URL. With your computer connected to the Internet this allows you to display a Web site during your presentation. Use this feature to show your company's Web site or to bring up an image or data on another site to help support your presentation's point.

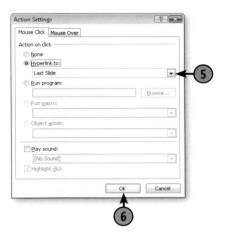

Tip ✓

Note that there are two tabs in the Action Settings dialog box, Mouse Click and Mouse Over. Depending on which tab you use to make settings, the action is initiated by you clicking on the object or by simply passing your mouse over the object during the presentation.

Tip ✓

After you draw a shape on your slide, you can just click on it and begin typing to add text.

Add a Text Box

① Click the Insert tab.

② Click the Text Box button. Your cursor changes to a plus symbol.

③ Click and drag on the slide to draw the text box, which remains open for editing.

④ Type text, and then click outside the box to close it.

Tip

You can format a text box. Right-click on the text and choose Format Shape. In the Format Shape dialog box that appears, use the various categories of settings to add fill color, an outside border, 3-D and rotation effects, and more. Once you draw a shape, when you select it a Drawing Tools, Format tab becomes available, which you can also use to make formatting changes.

See Also

In addition to adding action buttons on your slides, you can use effects such as animations and transitions to make your presentation more dynamic. See Section 11 for more about working with animations and transitions on slides.

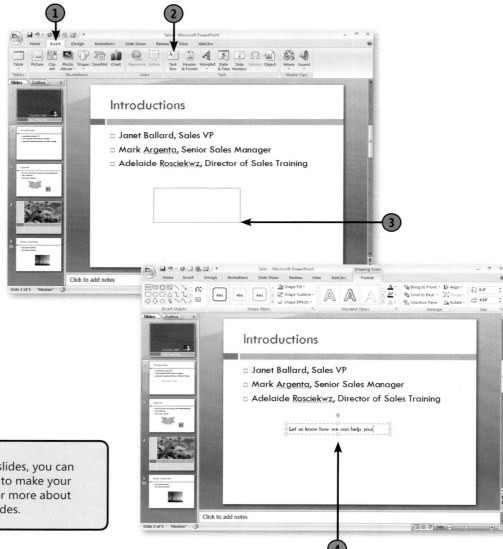

9

Formatting Text, Objects, and Slides

In this section:

- Applying Fonts
- Formatting Text
- Formatting Objects
- Resizing Objects
- Rotating Objects
- Grouping and Changing the Order of Objects
- Using Picture Tools
- Changing Slide Backgrounds

One of the hallmarks of a good presentation is consistency in look and feel. If there are elements you want to use consistently from slide to slide, such as a company logo, Masters can help you avoid having to add them again and again, slide after slide.

If you have selected a Theme for your slides, a set of font styles and colors have already been applied, but sometimes you may want to modify those styles or format a portion of the text for emphasis.

Placing a picture, a piece of line art, or a drawing on a slide helps you add some interest to your slides, but it's important that you make the object fit into your overall design. That may mean resizing or rotating the object to fit better with other elements on the slide, or modifying the color or brightness of the image to match your slide color scheme.

Finally, it may be useful to group objects that you insert on your slide so you can move or modify them as one object, or to set an order for objects so that one appears on top of another if they overlap.

In this chapter you explore the many ways you can format text and objects in PowerPoint, as well as resizing, rotating, grouping, and ordering those objects.

Applying Fonts

Fonts are design styles for text, and they add a distinct personality to your slide contents. Some fonts are playful, others are traditional, and still others are great for adding emphasis. The trick to choosing the right font for a presentation is to make sure it fits the design mood of your slides, and that it is readable by your audience in whatever setting you will show your presentation.

Select a Font

1. Click the Home tab.
2. Select the text you want to format.
3. Click the arrow on the Font field.

(continued on the next page)

(continued on the next page)

Tip

The fonts you see on the font list are those that come installed in Office 2007. You can find additional font sets online, some free and some that you have to pay for. Visit the Microsoft Typography Web site at www.microsoft.com/typography/default.mspx to learn more about fonts and find additional font sets.

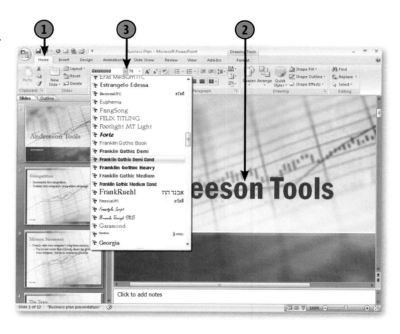

Select a Font *(continued)*

④ Move your mouse cursor down the list of fonts. Each font is previewed on the selected text in turn as you move your mouse through the list.

⑤ Click the font you want to apply in the list.

Try This!

You can also use the Font dialog box to change the font; however, there is no preview of the font appearance using this method. Click the dialog launcher icon in the Font group of tools on the Home tab to open the dialog box and click the arrow in the Latin Text Font drop-down list to display the font list. Choose the font you want and then click OK to apply it. The main benefit to using the Font dialog box is the ability to apply several formatting settings, such as size, font, and a bold effect, at one time.

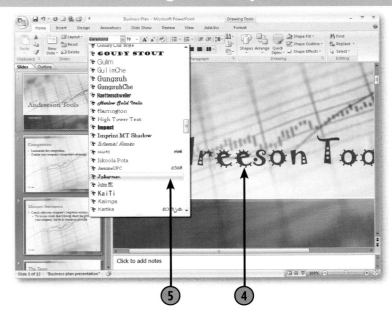

Formatting Text

There are several things you can do to help make your text more interesting or more easily readable, including resizing it, changing its color, or applying effects such as bold, italic, or underline. Design themes will apply preset font size and color, but when you want to fit more text on a page or emphasize some text, resizing is handy; and when you want to emphasize certain text, changing its color or making it bold, for example, can make it stand out.

Change Text Color

1. Click the Home tab.

2. Select the text you want to format.

3. Click the Font Color tool.

4. Move your mouse cursor over the colors in the palette to preview them in the selected text.

5. Click the More Colors option to view additional color choices.

(continued on the next page)

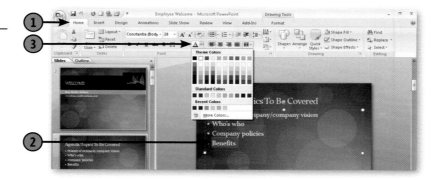

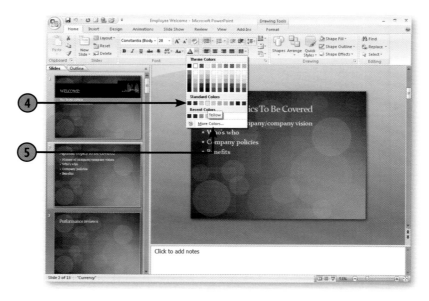

Change Text Color *(continued)*

6 Click either the Standard or Custom tab.

7 Click a color choice. Note that the Custom tab offers a Red/Green/Blue (RGB) color system that provides many more color choices and lets you make specific RGB settings.

8 Click OK to close the Color dialog box and apply the new color.

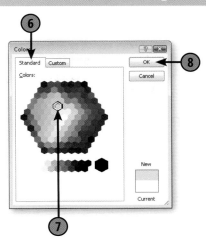

Tip

Be careful about choosing lighter colors that are hard to read unless your slides have a dark background against which they can stand out. Likewise, don't choose dark font colors against a dark background. Remember, the whole point of your presentation is to be readable by its viewers!

Tip

You can use the contextual toolbar that appears when you select text to change the font size and color or apply effects.

See Also

To change the background color of your slides so it works with your font color choices, see "Changing the Slide Background" on page 141.

Change Text Size

① Click the Home tab.

② Select the text you want to resize.

③ Click the arrow on the Font Size tool.

④ Move your cursor over the sizes; they are previewed on the selected text.

⑤ Click on a size to apply it.

Try This!

Not every single font size is available on the font size list. Only very commonly used sizes are included. If you find you need a size somewhere in between the preset ones, you can also type a size, such as 100, 13, or 30, in the font size box to apply it.

Tip

Don't make fonts so small they are difficult to read. Also note that as you add text to a placeholder, font sizes may shrink to fit all the text in. By keeping font sizes large enough to read and keeping your placeholder text to no more than six or so short bullet points, you ensure that your viewers can see your presentation's contents clearly.

Apply Effects to Text

① Click the Home tab.

② Select the text you want to format.

③ Click any of the following buttons to apply that format to the selected text:

- ■ Bold
- ■ Italic
- ■ Underline
- ■ Strikethrough
- ■ Shadow

④ Click the arrow on the Character Spacing button.

⑤ Click the spacing you prefer, from Very Tight to Very Loose. Very tight spacing pushes letters close together while very loose spacing places them further apart.

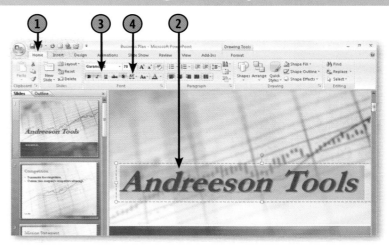

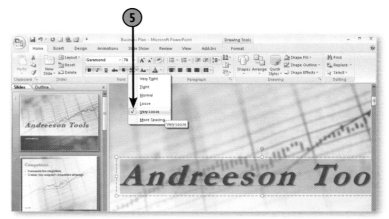

Try This!

To create custom character spacing, click the More Spacing option on the Character Spacing list. In the Font dialog box that appears, on the Character Spacing tab, choose expanded or condensed from the Spacing list, and then specify by how many points this effect should be applied. Click OK to save the new setting.

Tip

Character spacing is also known as *kerning*. In the Font dialog box on the Character Spacing tab you can specify that the kerning you apply be used only for fonts of a certain size and above by selecting the Kerning For Fonts checkbox and selecting a font size.

Tip

Note that you can apply multiple effects to text, such as bold plus italic plus shadow, but don't go overboard, or you'll make the text too busy to read!

Formatting Objects

Objects, including clip art, WordArt, pictures, and shapes that you draw on your slides, can all be formatted in several ways. You can fill an object with color or a pattern, change the outline of the shape by modifying the line style and thickness, and apply a wide variety of effects such as softening the edges or applying a 3-D rotation effect. Together these formatting options let you customize an object to make it appear just the way you want it to.

Apply a Fill Color or Effect

① Select a shape, text box, or WordArt object.

② Click the Drawing Tools, Format tab.

③ Click the Shape Fill button.

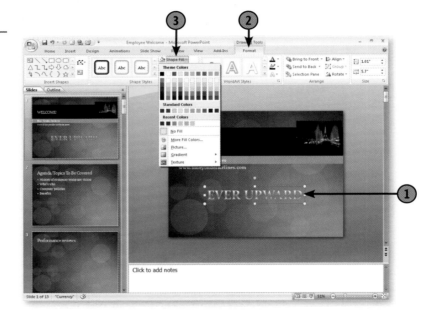

Apply a Fill Color or Effect *(continued)*

④ Use the Shape Fill gallery to make the changes you want to the selected object.

Try This!

The Fill gallery uses the new Live Preview feature. When you pass your mouse cursor over a Theme or Standard color, or over a Gradient or Texture option, it previews on the object on your slide.

Tip

You cannot add fill to clip art or a picture object because their "fill" is the image they contain. However, you can change their shape or border, or add effects such as 3-D. See those tasks elsewhere in this section to learn how to do this.

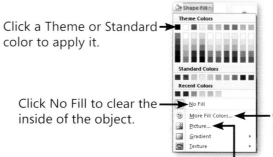

Click a Theme or Standard color to apply it.

Click No Fill to clear the inside of the object.

Click More Fill Colors to display a dialog box offering custom color options.

Click Picture to open a dialog box you can use to locate a picture to insert in the object.

Click Gradient or Texture to display a submenu of choices. Gradients give the impression of light sources coming from various directions, and textures range from water drops to a crinkled paper bag.

Change the Shape Outline

① Click an object to select it.

② Click the Format tab.

③ Click the Picture Border or Shape Outline button (depending on whether you've selected a picture or other type of object).

④ Use the gallery to make the changes you want to the selected object.

Tip

The Arrow option on the Shape Outline or Picture Border palette is only available if you are working with a line object.

See Also

If you want to format a placeholder rather than an object, see "Formatting Placeholders" on page 51.

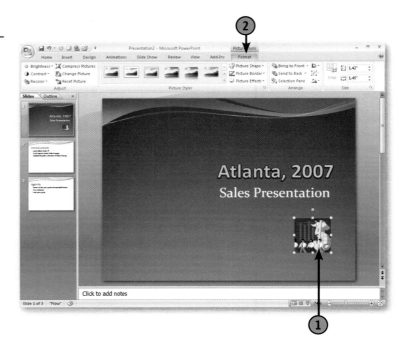

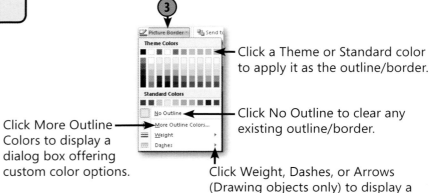

Click a Theme or Standard color to apply it as the outline/border.

Click No Outline to clear any existing outline/border.

Click More Outline Colors to display a dialog box offering custom color options.

Click Weight, Dashes, or Arrows (Drawing objects only) to display a submenu of formatting choices for the border/outline line.

Apply a Shape Effect

1. Click an object to select it.

2. Click the Format tab.

3. Click the Picture Effects or Shape Effects button (depending on whether you've selected a picture or other type of object).

4. Move your mouse over a category of effect and then click on an effect in the drop down gallery that appears.

5. PowerPoint applies the effect.

6. Repeat steps 3 and 4 to apply additional effects to the object.

Tip

You can apply more than one effect to an object. For example, you might choose to add a shadow, a reflection, and 3-D effect to one image. Just remember that you have to apply these effects one by one, using the steps outlined here.

Try This!

You can click the Format Shape dialog box launcher in the Shape Styles group to open the Format Shape dialog box. From here you can make all kinds of effect settings for the selected object from one place. When you are done applying effects, click Close, and they are all applied.

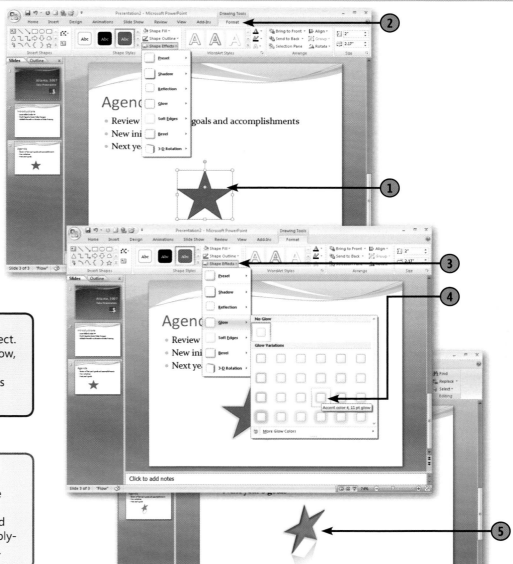

Resizing Objects

When you insert an object, it may not fit exactly as you'd like on your slide alongside other objects or placeholders. In that case, you can resize the object easily using resizing handles that appear when you click the object. Dragging corner handles resizes the object while maintaining its original proportions; dragging handles on the sides of the object resizes it but does not maintain the original proportions. This can cause it to appear somewhat distorted, like the image in a funhouse mirror.

Resize Objects

① Click on the object you want to resize.

② Click on a handle and drag inward to shrink the object or drag outward to enlarge it.

③ To resize the object to a specific measurement, click the Format tab.

④ Use the arrows on the Shape Height and Shape Width settings in the Size group of tools to set a specific measurement.

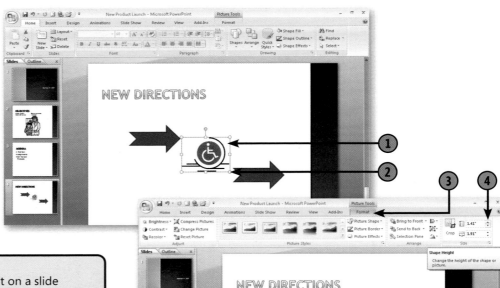

See Also

Sometimes rotating an object helps you to fit it on a slide among other objects. See the next task, "Rotating and Flipping Objects," to learn how to rotate an object.

Tip

If a picture is too large for your slide, consider cropping it using the Crop tool on the Format tab. This allows you to trim out unneeded portions of the picture, thereby saving space without reducing the picture size which might make it hard to see.

Rotating and Flipping Objects

Being able to rotate objects on your page can help you make interesting design arrangements on your slides or organize objects so they fit together. Rotating is easy to do using a rotation handle that appears whenever you click on an object. By clicking and dragging, you can rotate the object anywhere along a 360-degree axis.

Rotate an Object

① Click the object to select it and notice the green rotation handle that appears above it.

② Click on the rotation handle and while holding down your mouse button, spin the object. When the object appears at the angle you desire, release your mouse.

③ To rotate the selected object precisely 90°, click the Home tab.

④ Click the arrow on the Arrange button.

⑤ Click Rotate and choose Rotate Right 90° or Rotate Left 90° from the submenu.

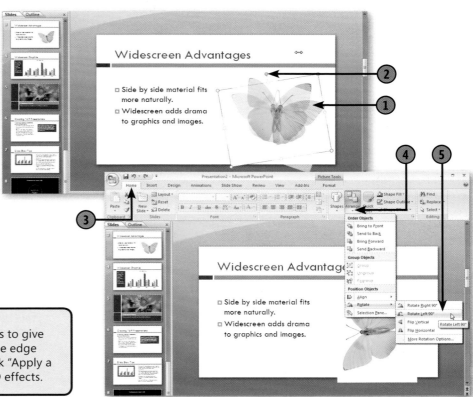

See Also

You can apply 3-D rotation effects that rotate objects to give them perspective, as if they were rotated to place one edge further in space from you than the other. See the task "Apply a Shape Effect" on page 133 to learn how to apply 3-D effects.

Tip

For more rotation options, click More Rotation Options in the Rotate menu. In the Size and Position dialog box that appears, you can enter specific measurements for height and width, as well as for setting the distance of the object from the edges of the slide.

Flip an Object

① Select the object and click the Home tab.

② Click the Arrange button.

③ Click Rotate and choose Flip Vertical or Flip Horizontal from the submenu. The action previews on the slide.

④ The object is flipped 180 degrees.

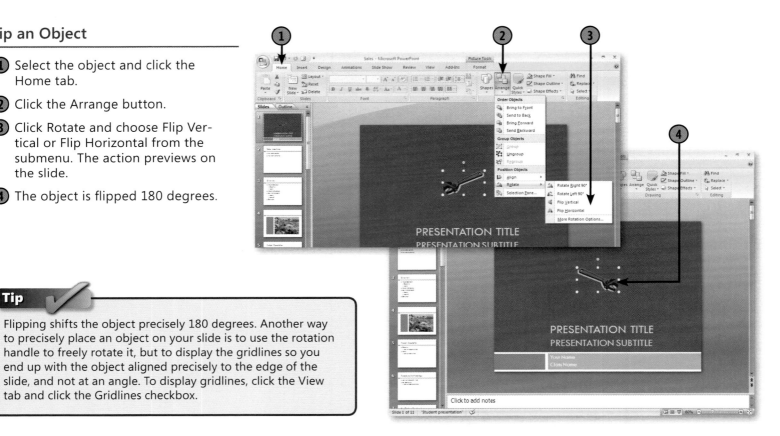

Grouping and Changing the Order of Objects

There are two handy functions that help you work with objects on your slide. Grouping allows you to group several objects, such as the different objects that form a drawing or logo, together into a single object. You can then work with that single object to format, move, or resize it. Also, when you have several objects on a slide they may overlap each other, either to save space or to create a design effect. In that case you should know how to control the order of objects on a page, that is, which object appears on top and which seems to fall underneath another.

Group and Ungroup Objects

1. Click an object to select it.

2. Press Ctrl and click on one or more other objects you want to group together.

3. Click the Drawing Tools, Format tab or Picture, Format tab, depending on the type of object.

4. Click the Group button and choose Group.

5. To ungroup the objects, select the grouped object, click the Group button, and then click Ungroup.

Tip

A grouped object has one outline surrounding all the objects and a single rotation handle. After objects are grouped, you can resize, move, rotate, and change the fill color of all objects at once, and so on.

Tip

To quickly select multiple objects on a slide, click and drag across them; a highlighted box surrounds the objects. Release your mouse, and all objects within the area you highlighted will be selected (not including placeholders).

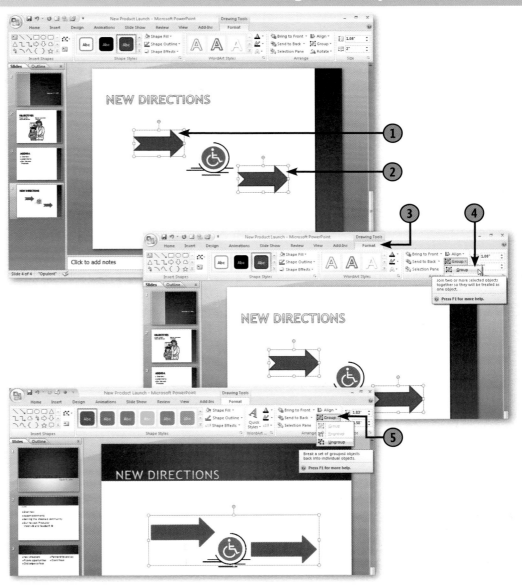

Change Object Order

 Click on an object to select it.

 Click the Drawing Tools, Format tab or Picture Tools, Format tab, depending on the type of object you're working with.

 Click the Bring to Front or Send to Back button to position the object at the very bottom or very top of any series of objects it overlaps.

See Also

For more information about inserting objects on your slides, see Section 8.

Tip

You can click the arrow on either the Bring to Front or Send to Back button and choose Bring Forward or Send Backward if you want to move an object only one position forward or backward in a stack of objects, rather than all the way to the front or back of the stack.

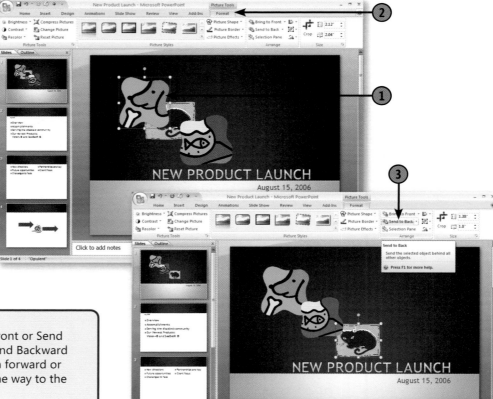

Working with Picture Tools

Because pictures have attributes such as brightness and contrast, they have their own special set of tools you can use to make adjustments to the images. By using these tools you can make pictures that are too dark appear brighter and pictures that are hard to see crisper by adjusting the contrast between darks and lights. You can also recolor pictures to apply a wash of light or dark color to them.

Adjust Brightness or Contrast

① Click a picture to select it.

② Click the Picture Tools, Format tab.

③ Click the Brightness or Contrast button.

④ Select a percentage from the list that appears. A plus number raises the brightness level or contrast, and a negative number reduces each. The effects are previewed on the picture as you move your mouse over the options.

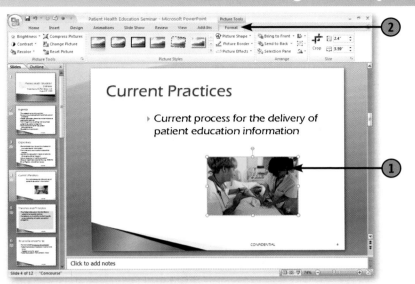

Tip ✓

If you want to work with both brightness and contrast settings at once, you can click Picture Corrections Options at the bottom of either the Brightness or Contrast list. This displays the Format Shape dialog box, with the Picture settings displayed. Your changes will still be previewed on the image for you as you make settings in this dialog box.

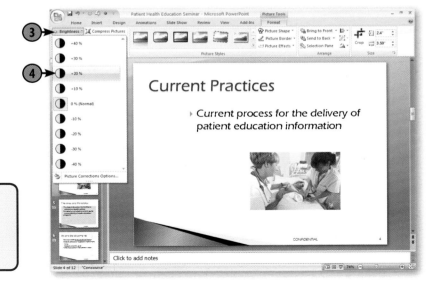

Tip ✓

The Photo Album feature is new to PowerPoint 2007. It allows you to create groups of photos to help you organize your images. See "Creating a Photo Album" on page 118 for more about Photo Album.

Recolor a Picture

1. Click a picture to select it.

2. Click the Picture Tools, Format tab.

3. Click the Recolor button.

4. Move your cursor around any Color Mode, Dark Variation, or Light Variation option to preview it.

5. Click on an option to apply it.

Tip

You can click the Set Transparent Color on the Recolor button menu. This causes the portion of the image that you drag over with your mouse to seem to disappear, revealing any objects underneath.

Caution

Be careful how you recolor pictures. Although coloring a picture may add some interest, it may also make the picture difficult to see in certain settings. Consider instead applying a colored border or slide background to add visual interest to a picture.

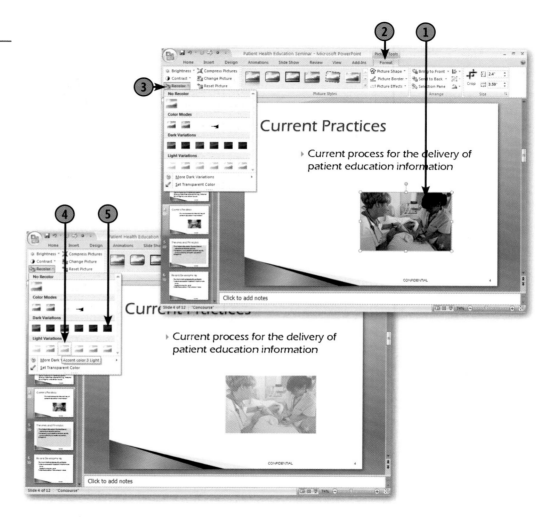

Changing the Slide Background

If you choose a slide theme a background is automatically applied, but you might want to apply a background of your own choosing. A background can be a solid color, or an effect such as a gradient (which makes it appear as if there is a light source shining on the background from various directions), or even a picture or texture. Backgrounds help make objects and text on the page stand out and add color and interest to your slides.

Change the Background Style

① Display the slide whose background you want to change.

② Click the Design tab.

③ Click the Background Styles button.

④ Click on a style to apply it.

Try This!

You can also customize a background by clicking Format Background at the bottom of the Background gallery. In the Format Background dialog box that appears, choose the type of fill you want to apply (Solid, Gradient, or Picture Or Texture Fill) and choose the settings for that type of background.

Tip

You can use the Hide Background Graphics checkbox in the Format Background dialog box to hide objects you have placed on slides from the Master Slide. See Section 10 for more about Slide Masters.

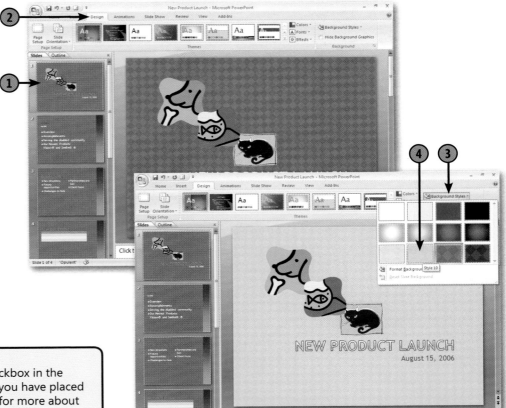

10

Working with Slide Masters

In this section:

- **Understanding How Slide Masters Work**
- **Making Changes to a Slide Master**
- **Adding and Deleting Master Sets**
- **Working with Handout and Notes Masters**

One of the hallmarks of a good presentation is consistency in look and feel. To achieve that consistency, you can use themes and color schemes built right into PowerPoint (see Section 7 for more about these). But there may be other elements you want to use consistently from slide to slide, such as a company logo, and it can be cumbersome to have to add these again and again, slide after slide.

That's where masters come in. Masters allow you to add a graphic, modify the text formatting or slide layout, or add a global footer. Then, whatever you have added in the master will appear on every slide.

Masters are flexible, as well. If you want one section of your presentation to use a master element or two, but in another section you want to introduce a change, you can use more than one master in your presentation to do so.

There are three masters you can work with in PowerPoint: Slide master, Handout master, and Notes master. Note that any changes you make on individual slides override the settings on masters.

Understanding How Slide Masters Work

Slide masters start out with a set of slide layouts defined by the currently applied theme template. That theme determines the font treatment, placement and size of placeholders, background graphics, animation, and color scheme. You can make changes to any of the layouts in a slide master, so that any time you apply one of those layouts to a slide, whatever is on that layout will appear automatically. You can use the Edit Master tools on the Slide Master tab to add a master set or add a new layout to an existing master set. Use Edit Theme tools on the Slide Master tab to change formatting for the text on your slides.

Slide Master tab

Master Layout thumbnail

Master Footer

Slide Master view

Master graphic

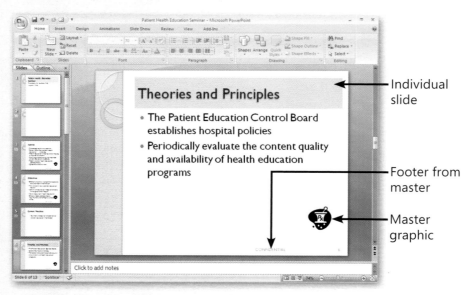

Individual slide

Footer from master

Master graphic

Making Changes to a Slide Master

Within the Slide Master view, you can work with font formats and bullet list styles, insert text or text boxes, add graphics, or rearrange elements of any slide layout. You make these changes much as you do in the Normal view of Power-Point. However, any changes you make in the Master view will be reflected on every slide to which the changed layout is applied. If you want to apply changes to all slides except the Slide Title layout, make those changes to the Master Layout at the top of the layout thumbnails.

Display and Navigate Masters

(1) Click the View tab and choose Slide Master from the Presentation Views group.

(2) Click and drag the vertical scrollbar on the left pane to view more layouts in the master.

(3) Click and drag the divider between panes if you want to see more or less of either pane.

(4) To exit Slide Master, click the Normal or Slide Sorter view button.

Try This!

Make changes to the Slide Master, and then save the presentation as a template (.potx). You can then base future presentations on that template. That way you only have to set up your company standard logo, colors, and so on once and then use the template again and again.

Tip ✓

The Zoom slider in the bottom right corner of the PowerPoint 2007 screen is new. You can use it to zoom in and out of the currently displayed layout in Slide Master's Slide pane.

Insert Footer Information

① With Slide Master displayed, click a footer placeholder to select it. Note one placeholder contains the current date by default.

② Enter whatever text you want in the placeholder; if you wish to move the footer placeholder, drag it wherever you wish on the slide and drop it.

③ A slide number element is included. If you don't want to use it, select it and press Delete on your keyboard to get rid of it, or drag the element to another location on the slide and drop it.

Tip

If you delete placeholders in a layout and want to put it back the way it was, in Slide Master click the layout to select it, click the Slide Master tab, and then click the Footers checkbox, and all original footer placeholders are reinstated.

Tip

The date footer is set to update automatically to reflect the date when you run the presentation. If you don't want the current date, delete the current date and type in a specific fixed date for each slide layout where you want it to appear. If you prefer this footer to reflect the date and time, or simply the time, use the Date and Time button on the Insert menu to do so.

Work with Master Graphics

(1) With the Slide Master displayed, select the layout you want to place the graphic on (for example the title slide or a content slide), and click the Insert tab. If you want to insert the graphic on every layout except the Slide Title layout, click the top-level Slide Master.

(2) Use the controls in the Illustrations group to insert a master graphic in your presentation:

- ■ Click to insert a picture.
- ■ Click to insert clip art.
- ■ Click to insert a chart.

(3) When you have inserted a graphic on the Slide Master, you can resize it or drag it to wherever you want it to be positioned and drop it.

> ### See Also
>
> See Section 8, "Inserting and Drawing Objects," for more about inserting pictures, clip art, and charts in your presentation; see "Resizing Objects" on page 134 for more about changing the size of objects.

> ### Caution
>
> When you place a master graphic, you typically put it in a corner of a slide so it doesn't overlap placeholder text or elements such as large tables. Still, if you use a graphic on every slide, the odds are it will overlap some object on a few slides in the presentation. Be sure to check for this and use the procedure in the task Omit Master Graphics on Individual Slides to move or remove the graphic on those individual slides.

Add a Layout

① With Slide Master view displayed, click the Slide Master tab and choose Insert Layout.

② On the new Custom Layout slide that appears, make any changes you like to the layout, such as:

- ■ Click to insert a new placeholder for any type of content.

- ■ Click an existing placeholder and press Delete.

- ■ Drag a placeholder to a new position on the slide.

Try This!

You can quickly and easily remove a Title or Footer placeholder from a layout. In the Master Layout group of tools on the Slide Master tab of the ribbon, just click the Title or Footers checkboxes. The item you deselect disappears from the current layout.

Tip

If you want to include or exclude an item from all slide layouts, use the Master Layout. Click the Master Layout thumbnail to display it, and then click the Master Layout button on the Slide Master tab. Click to display or remove items such as Title or Slide Number from all slides and click OK.

Omit Master Graphics on Individual Slides

(1) With the slide displayed in Normal view, click the Design tab of the ribbon to display it.

(2) Click the Hide Background Graphics checkbox in the Background group of tools.

(3) Repeat these two steps for any other slides where you want to omit master graphics.

Try This!

What if you have more than one master graphic and you want to omit one but not the others from an individual slide? You'll have to do this manually. Use the steps here to omit all master graphics and then insert the ones you want to use on the current slide one by one.

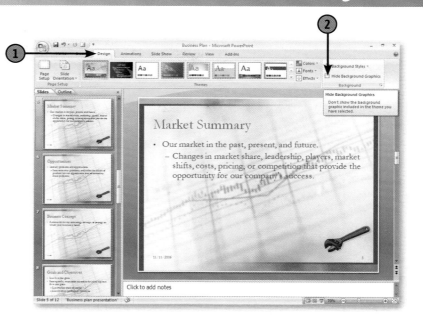

Adding and Deleting Master Sets

You can apply multiple themes to a single presentation. A set of master layouts is created whenever you apply an additional Theme template to your presentation. When you apply another theme to some of your slides, another set of thumbnails will appear in the left pane of the Slide master. You can also insert a new, blank master and then apply effects to it one by one to make a custom master.

If you have no more need for it, you can delete a master or rename it (for example, Company Logo Master) to make it easier to identify.

Rename a Master

1 With Slide Master view displayed, click the Master Layout slide for the master you want to rename.

2 From the Slide Master tab, click Rename in the Edit Master group of tools.

3 In the Rename Master dialog box, type a new name and click Rename.

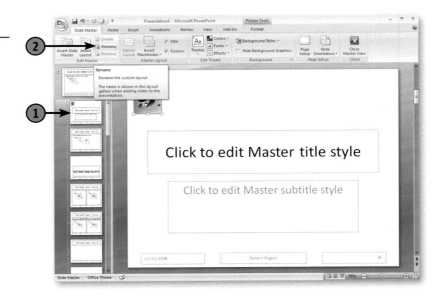

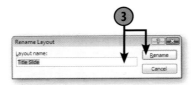

Delete a Master

1 With Slide Master view displayed, click the Master Layout slide for the master you want to delete.

2 Click the Home tab.

3 Click Delete in the Slides group of tools

Caution

If you delete a master from Slide Master, you can't undo the delete. You have to insert the master again by either applying a theme to slides or using the Insert Slide Master button in the Slide Master view.

See Also

For more information about applying themes to your presentation, see "Apply a Slide Theme" on page 80.

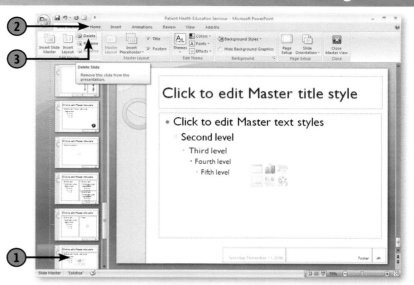

Insert Additional Masters

① To insert a blank master, with Slide Master view displayed, click the Slide Master tab and choose Insert Slide Master in the Edit Master group of tools.

② To insert an additional theme in your presentation, click Themes in the Edit Theme group of tools and click on the theme you want from the gallery that appears.

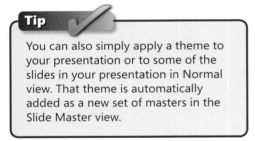

Tip

You can also simply apply a theme to your presentation or to some of the slides in your presentation in Normal view. That theme is automatically added as a new set of masters in the Slide Master view.

Working with Handout and Notes Masters

Handouts are essentially a printing option for PowerPoint. You can print one, two, three, four, six, or nine slides on a page and hand those pages out to your audience to follow along with your presentation, or to take with them as a reminder of key points. In the Handout master you can enter up to two headers and two footers, rearrange or delete placeholders, set the orientation of the handouts, and set the number of slides to print on a page.

Notes can be printed for the benefit of the person making the presentation, providing a handy reference while presenting. Notes consist of a slide along with an area for notes and placeholders for header and footer text. Notes can be entered in the Notes pane of Normal view. The Notes master allows you to arrange the placement of the various elements on the Notes page globally.

Work with Handout Master

① Click Handout Master in the Presentation Views group of the View tab.

② Do any of the following:

- Click in a placeholder and enter text or replace the date or slide number element already there.

- Drag a placeholder and drop it in a new location.

- Click to remove any of the four placeholders from handouts.

③ Click Slide Orientation or Handout Orientation and choose Portrait or Landscape.

④ Click Slides Per Page and choose an option from the drop-down gallery.

⑤ Click Background Styles and choose a background for the handouts from the drop-down gallery.

⑥ Click the various tools in the Edit Theme group to choose formatting options from the various drop- down galleries.

⑦ Click Close Master View when you're done with Handout master settings to return to Normal view.

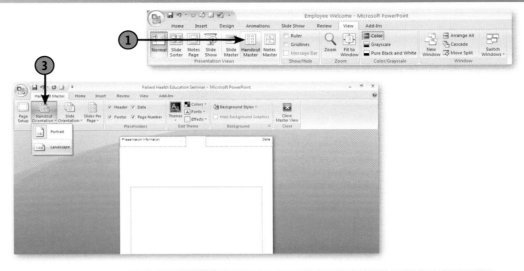

Try This!

You can use the Insert tab when in Handout Master to insert graphics that will only appear on your handouts. For example, you might want to insert a logo and the words "Company Confidential" on handouts to ensure that people treat the handouts as private.

Tip

To leave background graphics off of handouts, which can make the text easier to read, click the Hide Background Graphics checkbox in the Background group on the Handout Master tab.

Work with Notes Master

① Click Notes Master in the Presentation Views group of the View tab.

② Click in a placeholder and enter text or replace the date or slide number element already there.

③ Drag a placeholder and drop it in a new location.

④ Click to remove any of the six placeholders from handouts.

⑤ Click Slide Orientation or Notes Page Orientation and choose Portrait or Landscape.

(continued on the next page)

Tip

You can click and drag any placeholder to a new location.

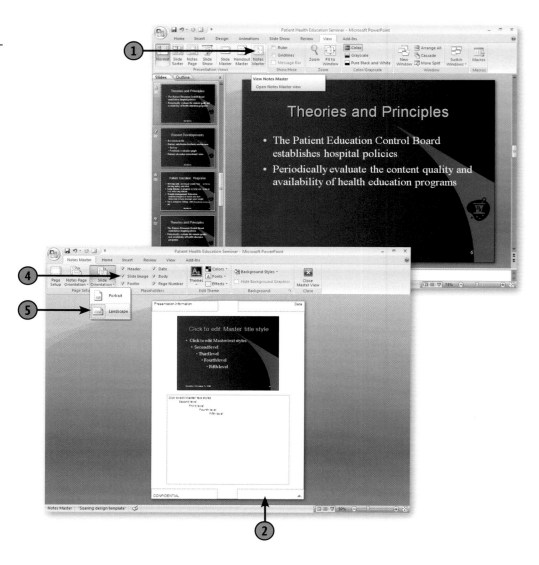

Work with Notes Master *(continued)*

6 Click to choose a background for the handouts from the Background Styles drop-down gallery.

7 Click the tools from the Edit Theme group to choose formatting options from the various drop-down galleries.

8 Click Close Master View when you're done with Notes Master settings to return to Normal view.

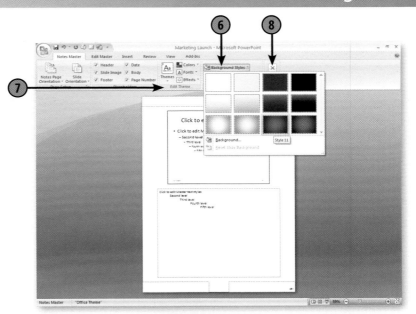

Tip ✓

Be sure to format the Notes body so you can easily read your notes while making a presentation, often in a darkened room. Make the font size large and use a font that is clean and easy to read.

See Also ➤

For more information about formatting text to make it easily readable, see "Formatting Text" on page 126.

11

Adding Transition Animations

In this section:

■ Applying a Transition to a Slide

■ Adding Sound to a Transition

■ Modifying Transition Speed

■ Choosing How to Advance a Slide

■ Applying a Custom Animation to Objects

■ Previewing an Animation

Animations in PowerPoint are used to transition from one slide to another when you are showing a slide presentation in Slide Show mode. They can also be applied to individual objects to cause them to appear on a slide with an animation effect such as spinning or seeming to grow on the slide.

The transition that takes effect when you move from one slide to another in a slide show can vary for each slide change or be applied globally. You can also control the speed of each transition, and even add a sound that is played along with the transition effect.

Using a custom animation effect to control how individual objects appear on your slide allows you to cause individual bullet points on a slide to appear in a timed sequence or only appear one by one as you click your mouse. You can even apply a motion path that causes an object to enter from a certain direction, move to one area of the slide, then move to another, and so forth.

Animations and transitions are a great way to draw attention or add visual interest to your presentation.

Applying a Transition

You can use a gallery of preset animations to apply a transition effect that occurs when a new slide appears. These transition effects are divided into categories such as Fades and Dissolves, or Stripes and Bars. You can apply a different effect between each pair of slides or one effect to occur every time a slide changes. The Random category of effects cycles among different styles in a random way.

Apply a Transition Scheme to a Slide

1. If you want a transition to occur when a particular slide appears, display that slide.

2. Click the Animations tab.

3. Click the More button on the Transitions gallery to display it.

4. Move your cursor over the various effects to see them previewed on your slide.

5. Click on a transition effect to apply it to that slide.

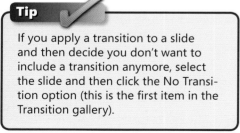

Tip

If you apply a transition to a slide and then decide you don't want to include a transition anymore, select the slide and then click the No Transition option (this is the first item in the Transition gallery).

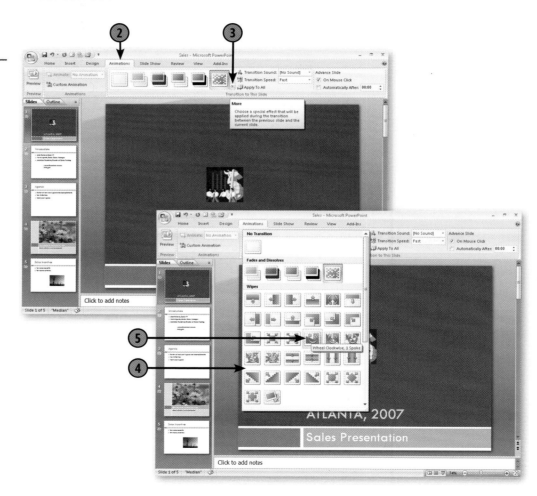

Apply a Transition to All Slides

① Click the Animations tab.

② Apply a transition scheme to a slide following the steps in the previous task.

③ Click the Apply to All button. Stars appear next to all slides in the slide pane to indicate the applied transition.

Tip

You can tell whether a transition or other animation effect is applied to a slide in a couple of ways. In Normal view a star icon appears to the left of the slide in the Slides pane. In the Slide Sorter view, the star icon appears below any slide that has an animation applied.

See Also

For more information about adding animations to individual objects on a slide, see "Applying a Custom Animation to an Object" on page 165.

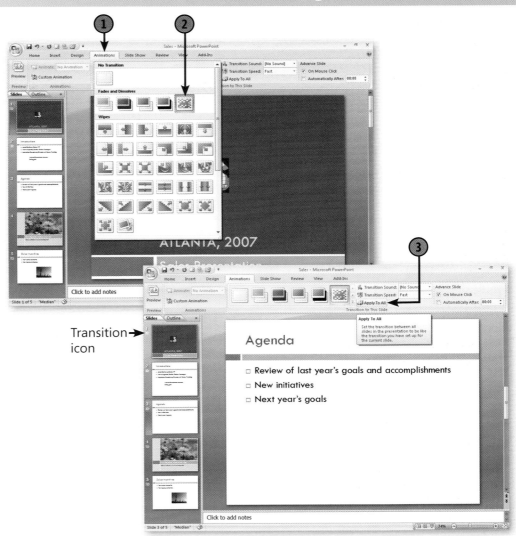

Transition→ icon

Adding Sound to Transitions

Imagine that you have set up a slide transition to occur that has the new slide appear to fly in from the left side. If you also added a sound effect like a burst of wind, it would add impact to the transition. That's what adding sounds to transitions is all about: Catching your audience's attention with a sound that complements the transition effect and the contents of the slide. You can also add sounds to custom animations on individual objects; so, when that Clip Art of a pile of money appears, why not have a cash register sound happen simultaneously?

Add Sound

① Select a slide with a transition applied to it and click the Animations tab.

② Click the Transition Sound field.

(continued on the next page)

See Also

You can also apply a sound to an object that has a custom animation applied to it by simply selecting the object before applying the sound. To learn more, see "Modify Animation Settings on page 166.

Add Sound (continued)

③ Move your cursor over the sounds in the list to preview them.

④ Click a sound to apply it to the current slide.

Try This!

If you want a sound to keep repeating until the next sound is played, click the Loop Until Next Sound option at the bottom of the Transition Sound list. Repeating a sound this way can be a great effect, but don't let it go on too long, or you'll drive your viewers crazy!

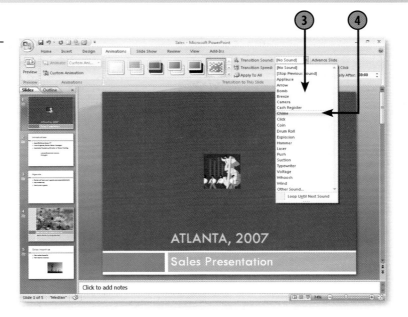

Modifying Transition Speed

Transitions can happen at a slow, medium, or fast speed. A fast transition between slides provides a little subconscious shift, but it's so fast most people don't notice the effect itself. A transition that happens slowly, on the other hand, is more noticeable to the viewers, but you run the danger of slowing down your presentation if you overuse them. The ability to control the speed of transitions is useful, but you will have to determine which speed fits each transition and your presentation best.

See Also

For information about setting the speed for custom animations applied to individual objects, see "Applying a Custom Animation to an Object" on page 165.

Caution

If you play a sound along with a transition, and you set the transition to run fast, the sound occurs quickly, too. In fact, the sound may happen so fast that it can be hard to tell what the sound is. If you use a sound like a typewriter, for example, associated with a fast transition, your viewers may hear a single click of a typewriter key—not enough to know what it is they are hearing!

Set the Speed for Transitions

1. Display a slide that has a transition applied to it and click the Animations tab if necessary.

2. Click the Transition Speed field.

③ Select Slow, Medium, or Fast.

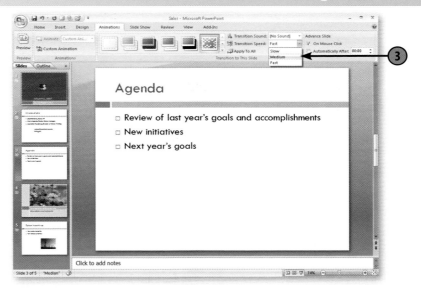

Tip

To use the transition speed that is applied to the currently selected slide on all the slides in your presentation, click the Apply to All button on the Animations tab.

Choosing How to Advance a Slide

You can advance from slide to slide in a presentation in several ways, such as clicking your mouse, or by waiting for a certain interval of time to pass. The manual approach of clicking your mouse gives you control, but keeps your hands busy during the presentation. The automatic timed advance feature is useful when you are showing a slide show on the Web or in an unattended setting, such as a mall kiosk. If you need to have a combination of methods within the presentation, you can make this setting on a slide by slide basis using tools on the Animations tab.

Select a Method to Advance a Slide

① Display a slide with a transition applied to it.

② Click the Animations tab.

③ Click the On Mouse Click check box to advance the slide manually; or...

④ Click the Automatically After check box.

⑤ Click the spinner arrows to set an interval of time at which to advance.

See Also

For more about navigating through a slide show presentation, see "Navigating through Slides" on page 191.

Tip

You can also use the right arrow on your keyboard to advance a presentation, if you have the keyboard handy, or click the Slide tool that appears in Slide Show view and choose Next or Previous from the pop-up menu.

See Also

You can set up your show so that all slides are advanced using the same method. For information on how to make this setting, see "Select a Method to Advance a Slide" on page 164.

Applying a Custom Animation to an Object

You can apply custom animations to individual objects on your slide, from clip art and pictures to text placeholders. Animations include effects that make an object seem to appear on or disappear from your slide in Slide Show view in some fash-ion. For example, you might choose to have a heading appear letter by letter, or fly off your slide. The Motion Path category of animation allows you to actually have the object appear and move around a path you specify on your slide.

Add an Animation Effect to an Object

① Click the object to select it.

② Click the Animations tab.

③ Click the Custom Animation button to display the Custom Animation task pane listing all animations for the currently displayed slide.

④ Click the Add Effect button.

⑤ Click a category of effect and then click an effect from the side menu that appears.

Try This!

If you want the same custom animation applied to all objects of a certain type, for example, to all title objects on slides using a title and content layout, apply the custom animation in the Slide Master view.

Tip

Don't overdo custom animations. If they play all the time your audience will become bored with them. Use them for special emphasis, at the start of a new section of your presentation, or to drive home a key point.

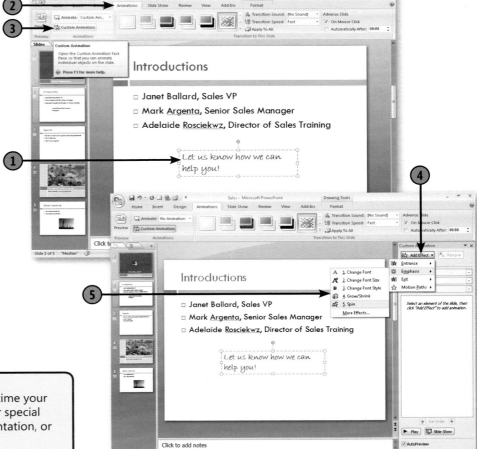

Modify Animation Settings

1 Display a slide that has an object with an animation effect applied to it.

2 Click the Animations tab.

3 Click Custom Animation to display the Custom Animation task pane.

4 Click on the animation you want to modify in the list.

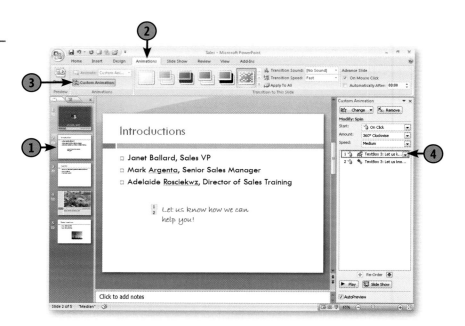

You can also click the arrow to the right of the effect in the list of effects and choose Effect Options from the menu that appears to make all these settings and more in a dialog box. If you select the option of starting an animation after another animation plays, you can use the Timing tab of this dialog box to specify a delay between the two animations, if you wish.

(5) Click the Start field and choose whether the effect plays when you click your mouse, along with any previous animation, or after the previous animation.

(6) Click the next field, which will have a different name depending on the effect you have chosen, and make the appropriate setting. For example, if your effect shrinks your text, this Font Size field lets you choose the font size to shrink to. If your effect causes the object to spin, this Amount field lets you choose how many degrees around the object should spin.

(7) Click the Speed field and choose how quickly the effect should play.

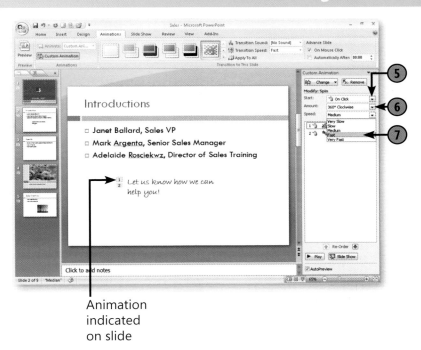

Animation
indicated
on slide

Tip

To remove an animation effect from an object, click on it in the list of effects in the Custom Animation task pane and click the Remove button.

Reorder Effects

① With the Custom Animation task pane displayed (click the Custom Animation button on the Animations tab), click on an effect in the list.

② Click Move Up to move the effect up in the list.

③ Click Move Down to move the effect down in the list.

④ Repeat steps 1, 2, and 3 to reorganize the list of effects in any way you like.

Tip

If you reorganize slides, remember to check the Start setting you gave each. For example, if you wanted a slide to use a certain entrance effect that related to the contents of the slide before it, when you move that slide you may want to change the entrance effect to be relevant to its new predecessor.

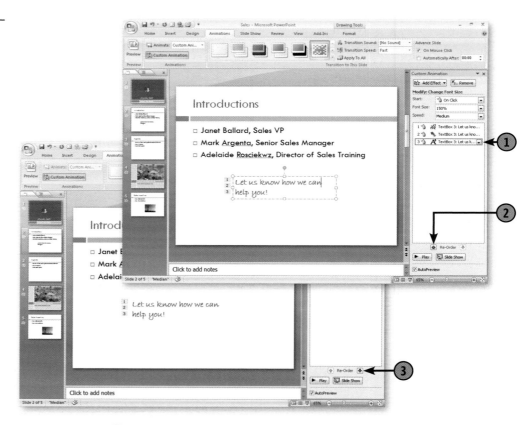

Tip

Note that you can apply more than one animation to any object. So you might have a heading shrink font size, spin around 360°, and then fly off the slide. If you do this, you can use the method described here to reorder the effects applied to that object.

Previewing an Animation

PowerPoint offers a couple of options for previewing an animation effect on a slide in Normal view. There is a Preview button on the Animation toolbar that plays all the effects on a slide, and the Custom Animation task pane offers a Play button to play the individual animations on the animation list. There is also a Slide Show button in this task pane to quickly go into Slide Show view.

Preview an Animation

1. With a slide containing animations displayed, click the Animations tab.

2. Click the Preview button.

3. Click the Custom Animation button.

4. Click the Play button to play the applied animations in sequence.

5. To view the animation in Slide Show view, click the Slide Show button at the bottom of the Custom Animation task pane.

6. To stop the preview from running, click the Stop button at any time.

Try This!

If you click the Play button in the Custom Animation task pane to preview the animations, a little timer bar appears at the bottom of the list. You can use this to tally up the seconds it takes for all your animations to play.

Tip

You can select the AutoPreview check box at the bottom of the Custom Animation task pane if you want to see a preview of each animation when you apply it to an object.

12

Finalizing Your Slide Show

In this section:

- **Proofing and Sending Your Presentation**
- **Setting Up Your Show**
- **Rehearsing Your Presentation**
- **Saving a Presentation to CD**

After you have put in all the effort to build a stunning presentation, composing the perfect content and choosing attractive design elements and graphics, you should take the time to proofread it to make sure you haven't made spelling or other errors. PowerPoint provides a spelling check feature to help you check your contents, as well as a thesaurus to help you find the perfect word. You can also send the presentation to be reviewed by other people, who can help you spot problems before you give the presentation in front of an audience.

At this point you should set up how your slide show will run. For example, will you be able to use multiple monitors, and will the presentation run in a continuous loop or just one time from beginning to end? This is also the time to rehearse your presentation to ensure that the slide show will run smoothly. While rehearsing a presentation, you can add a narration and timing that controls how long a slide is displayed. These are useful if the presentation will run on its own with no live presenter available.

Reviewing Your Presentation

When you finish adding the last sentence of text and final graphic object to your presentation, you're not quite done. Because your presentation is likely to be displayed on a large screen in front of many people, any error or glitch is likely to undermine the credibility of your message. For that reason, taking the time to check spelling, word choices, and the look of your contents is very important. PowerPoint provides tools to help you check the accuracy of your contents and offers the ability to send your presentation to others to review to make sure everything looks perfect. You can ask others to make changes or simply add comments with their suggestions for your review.

See Also

For information about viewing and moving slides around in your presentation, see "Viewing Slides in a Slide Pane" on page 66 and "Move a Slide" on page 70.

Tip

After working on your presentation for hours, days, or weeks, you are likely to be too close to it to spot problems. In addition to using PowerPoint's spelling check feature, be sure to have somebody objective read through the presentation, or if nobody else is available, read each sentence backward to proof it. When we read a sentence forward we make assumptions about the next word based on context. When we read from last word to first, each word and its spelling stands out, and any missing words may be more obvious.

Check Spelling

1. Open the presentation you want to review. If you want to check the spelling of a single word, select it.

2. Click the Review tab.

3. Click the Spelling button.

(continued on the next page)

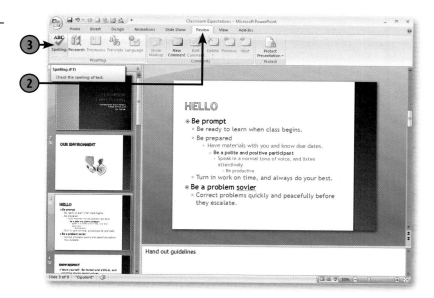

Check Spelling *(continued)*

4 Take any of the following actions:

- Click a spelling in the Suggestions list and then click Change or Change All to apply it to the current word or all instances of the word in your presentation, respectively.

- Enter a new spelling in the Change To field and click Change or Change All.

- Click Ignore or Ignore All to disregard this instance of the spelling or all instances of it in your presentation, respectively.

- Click Add to add the spelling to PowerPoint's dictionary.

- Click AutoCorrect if this is a mistake you commonly make and want it added to the Auto-Correct list to be corrected in future as you type.

5 When you click one of the above options, PowerPoint moves you to the next word that needs checking. When all errors have been checked, a dialog box appears telling you the spelling check is complete. Click OK.

Tip

To stop a manual spelling check at any time, just click the Close button in the Spelling dialog box.

Tip

PowerPoint is set up by default to check spelling automatically, which causes wavy colored lines to appear under words that have questionable spelling. To get rid of those wavy lines on your screen, click the Office button, then click PowerPoint Options, and select Proofing. Select the Hide Spelling Errors check box and then click OK.

Tip

If you right-click on a word and it has a possible spelling error, PowerPoint displays alternative spellings or words on the shortcut menu that appears. Just click on one to make the change.

Use the Thesaurus

(1) Display the slide that contains the word you want to check and select that word. If the word you want to check isn't in your presentation, skip this step.

(2) Click the Review tab.

(3) Click the Thesaurus button.

(4) If you did not select a word prior to clicking the Thesaurus button, enter a word in the Search For box.

(5) Click the Start Searching button to begin the search.

(continued on the next page)

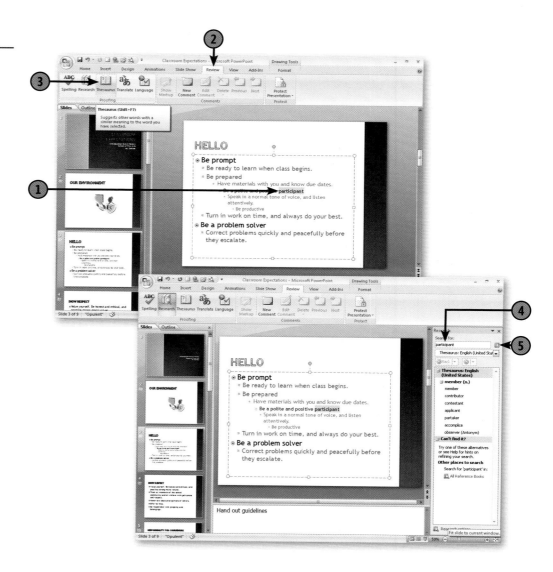

Use the Thesaurus *(continued)*

6 Click a word in the list of results to display additional similar words.

7 Click the Back button to move back to a previous list of words.

8 Click the arrow next to a selected word and choose Insert to have that word replace the selected word, or if no word was selected in Step 1, to insert the word in your slide.

9 Click the Close button in the Research task pane to close it.

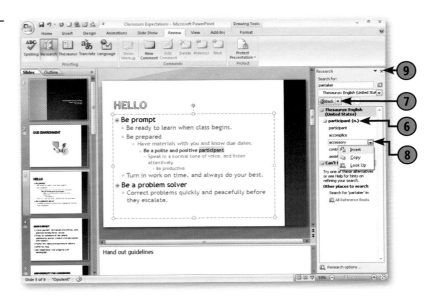

Tip

You can change which resources are searched by clicking the second field in the Search For section of the Research task pane and selecting different options. These mainly consist of different language dictionaries and, if you are online, encyclopedias, and other research sites.

Add Comments

1. Display a slide to which you want to add a comment.

2. If you want to attach a comment to a particular object or place-holder, click to select it.

3. Click the Review tab.

4. Click New Comment.

5. Type your comment and then click anywhere outside the comment box.

Try This!

Try using the tools in the Comments group on the Review tab to edit, delete, or cycle through comments in your presentation. To hide all comments from your view, click the Show Markup button.

Tip

Comments do not show in Slide Show or Slide Sorter view. They are intended mainly for reviewers to pass on comments on a presentation that is being created. If you want to include comments with your presentation, consider adding notes and printing the Notes view for your audience.

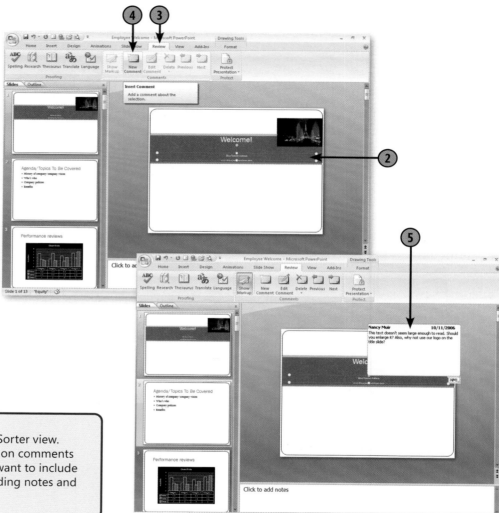

E-mail a Presentation for Review

(1) With the presentation open that you want to e-mail, click the Office button.

(2) Click Send.

(3) Click E-mail

(4) In the e-mail form that opens in your default e-mail program, type a recipient's e-mail address in the To field.

(5) Type a subject in the Subject field.

(6) Type the text of any message you want to send in the body of the message.

(7) Click Send.

Tip

The presentation will be attached as a PowerPoint file. If you are sending the presentation to somebody who doesn't have PowerPoint available, consider saving the presentation as a PowerPoint Show file. This format opens your presentation in Slide Show mode on any Windows computer; however, viewers will not be able to use reviewing features such as inserting comments.

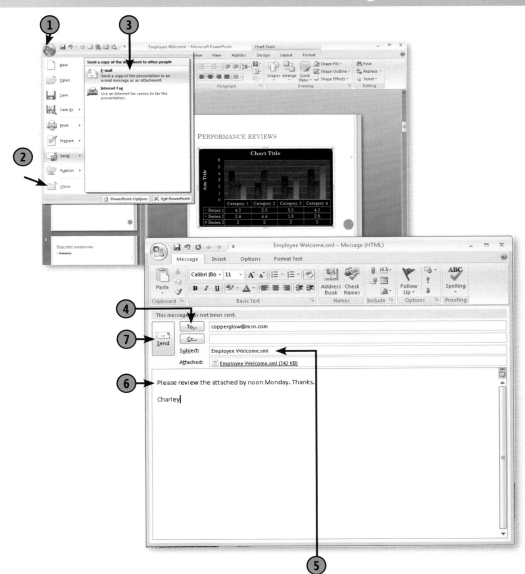

Setting Up a Slide Show

Several variables affect how your slide show will run. For example, you can set up a slide show to be presented by a live speaker or to be browsed by a viewer. You can specify that a show should loop continuously or be shown with or without a recorded narration. You can even choose to have only a subset of the slides in the presentation included in a particular slide show. You can set up your show to advance manually when a presenter clicks or automatically according to recorded timings. Finally, you can specify that more than one monitor will be used; with this feature the presenter can have one monitor to use to orchestrate the show while the audience sees the presentation on another monitor.

Set the Show Type

1. Click the Slide Show tab.

2. Click the Set Up Slide Show button.

3. Click one of the three radio buttons in the Show type section:

   - Presented By A Speaker displays the slide show in full screen mode and assumes a live presenter is running the show

   - Browsed By An Individual is the setting to use if an individual will view the show from a computer or CD. This presentation runs in a window, rather than full screen.

   - Browsed At A Kiosk provides a self-running, full screen presentation that might be set up at a kiosk.

4. Click OK to save your settings.

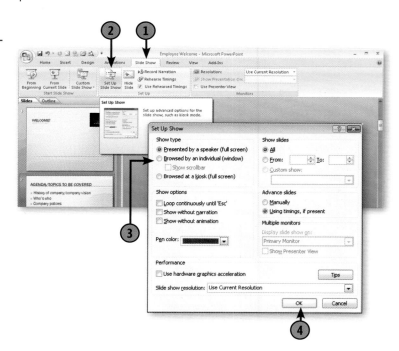

Try This!

Click the Show Scrollbar checkbox if you choose the Browsed By An Individual setting to enable a viewer to scroll through a presentation. This works well with a presentation that will run from a computer that is unattended, such as a computer showing a demonstration at a booth in a trade show.

Tip

If you want a show to play unattended, it's a good idea to loop it so that it repeats over and over again in your absence.

Specify Show Options

① Click the Slide Show tab.

② Click the Set Up Slide Show button.

③ Click one of the three check boxes in the Show options section:

- Loop Continuously Until 'Esc'. Choose this option if you are running the show unattended and want it to continuously repeat.

- Show Without Narration. If you recorded a narration but now want to give the show with a live presenter, you would choose this option.

- Show Without Animation. Because animations may not run smoothly on slower computers, you might choose to disable them using this setting.

④ Click the arrow on the Pen Color field and choose an ink color from the drop-down palette for annotations you can make while running a show.

⑤ Click OK to save your settings.

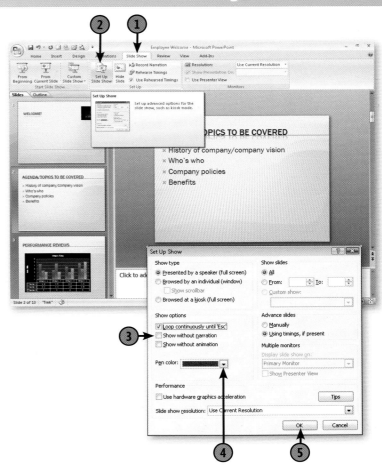

Tip

You can choose additional colors for the pen by clicking More Colors at the bottom of the drop-down palette. This displays the Colors dialog box, where you can select a Standard or Custom color to apply.

See Also

For information about working with the pen to make annotations during a presentation, see "Make Annotations on Slides" on page 195.

Specify Which Slides to Include

① Click the Slide Show tab.

② Click the Set Up Slide Show button.

③ In the Show Slides section, click a radio button to choose one of three options:

- Choose All to include all slides in the presentation (except for slides you've hidden).

- Enter beginning and ending slide numbers in the From and To field to show a range of slides.

- Use Custom Show to pick and choose any number or range of slides you wish to present. This feature enables you to present different versions of your show to different audiences.

④ Click OK to save your settings.

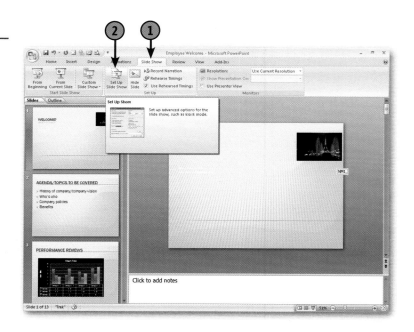

Try This!

If you have a large slide show and find it's running slowly on the presenting computer, don't shorten your show. Instead, you can adjust the Slide Show Resolution in the Set Up Show dialog box. A lower resolution such as 600 x 800 will run your slides faster, though the image quality will be grainier.

See Also

For information about working with custom shows, see "Creating a Custom Show" on page 217.

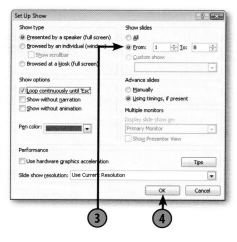

Set Up How to Advance Slides

1 Click the Slide Show tab.

2 Click the Set Up Slide Show button.

3 Click a radio button to choose how to advance slides:

- ■ Manually requires you to click a mouse, press an arrow on your keyboard, or use the navigation tools in Slide Show view.

- ■ Using Timings, If Present moves the slides forward automatically based on the timings you save when you rehearse.

4 Click OK to save your settings.

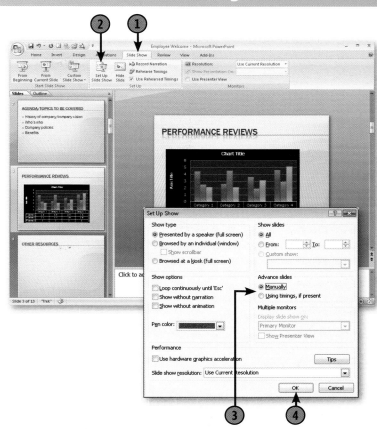

See Also

For more information about how to move from slide to slide in a presentation, see "Navigating through Slides" on page 191.

Tip

The Show Presenter View option is a setting in the Set Up Show dialog box that can come in handy if you have a system with multiple monitors. This is useful if you want to control the show from one screen, on your laptop for instance, but use another screen to display the presentation to your viewers. Using the Show Presenter View on your screen, you can navigate the slide show and your actions will be invisible to your viewers. For example, you can use thumbnails of your slides to build a custom presentation, reordering slides to offer a recap of key ideas on the fly.

Try This!

When you record a narration, you are offered the option of saving timings as well. If you do, those timings will be used to advance slides based on when the narration for each slide is complete. Note that there is a Use Rehearsed Timings check box on the Slide Show tab you can check to override narration timings.

Rehearsing Your Presentation

It's very important that you prepare for your presentation. Rehearsing has several benefits. First, during your rehearsal you can save timings that can be used to advance your slides automatically or record a narration. Even if you don't use those timings to navigate your presentation, they help you anticipate whether your presentation will go under or over the allotted time. In addition, rehearsing helps you spot problems in running your presentation, such as animations that take a long time to play or type that is hard to read.

Add a Narration

1. Attach a microphone to your computer.
2. Click the Slide Show tab.
3. Click Record Narration.
4. If you need to set the microphone level click Set Microphone Level.

(continued on the next page)

Try This!

You can adjust the quality of your microphone before you begin recording. Simply click the Change Quality button in the Record Narration dialog box, and in the Sound Selection dialog box that appears, choose different attributes. For example, choosing a higher kilohertz, higher bit, stereo setting should provide a higher sampling rate. This means your sound quality will be crisper and clearer.

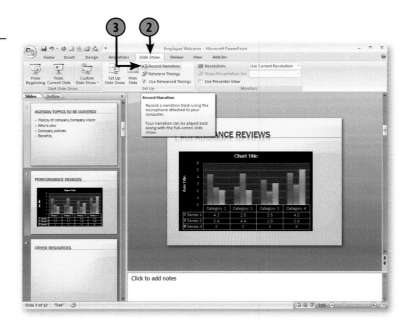

Add a Narration *(continued)*

⑤ Read the speech in the Microphone Check dialog box to check your level and then click OK.

⑥ In the Record Narration dialog box, click Current Slide to begin the presentation from the currently displayed slide or First Slide to start at the beginning.

⑦ The Slide Show view displays. Begin reading your narration, advancing your slides as you would during a slide show.

⑧ When you reach the end, click Save to save the timings along with the narration, or Don't Save if you don't want to save them.

Tip

Your sound quality will be better if you have a more sensitive microphone. It might be worth spending a bit more for a better microphone headset to provide quality recording. Typically, there is a microphone or headset outlet on the back or front of your computer for plugging these in, and no other special hardware is required.

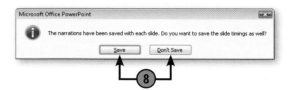

Save Timings

(1) Click the Slide Show tab.

(2) Click Rehearse Timings.

(3) Navigate through your slide show, leaving each slide on for the approximate length of time you wish to display it and discuss its contents.

(4) When the slide show is done, in the dialog box that displays the total time for the show, click Yes to keep the settings or No to discard them.

(5) Saved timings will appear underneath slides in the Slide Sorter view.

See Also

For more information about running your slide show, see the tasks "Navigating through Slides" on page 191 and "End a Show" on page 190.

Tip

If you add to or change the content of your presentation in any way, you may want to change the saved timings. To save new timings simply run the Rehearse Timings feature again and save the timings. Only one set of timings at a time can be saved with your slides.

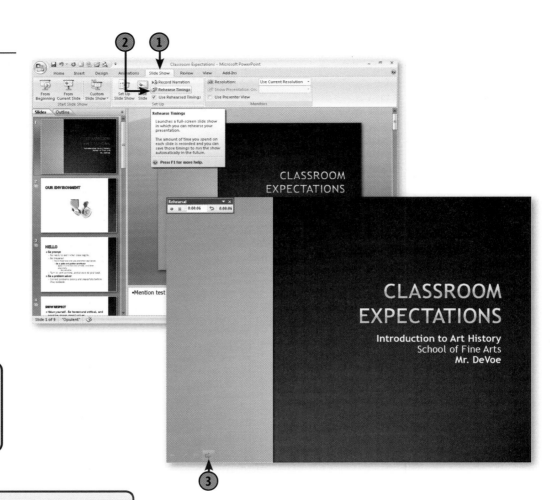

Taking a Presentation with You

Most of the time you will not give a presentation where you designed it, but instead you will take it on the road, whether the locale is in a meeting room two doors down or in another state or country. To do this, you save a presentation to some media such as a CD. When you publish your presentation to media in this way, you can also add the PowerPoint Viewer so that you can run the presentation even on a computer that doesn't have PowerPoint installed.

Save a Presentation to CD

1. Insert a CD in your computer's CD recorder drive.
2. Click the Office button.
3. Click Publish.
4. Click Package For CD.
5. If a dialog appears asking whether you want to update some elements to compatible file formats, click OK.
6. In the Package for CD dialog box that appears, enter a name for the CD.
7. If you want to add more files, such as files you need for background information, click Add Files and select them. (Note that linked files are included by default.)
8. Click Copy To CD.
9. Click Yes in the message that appears asking whether you want to include linked files.

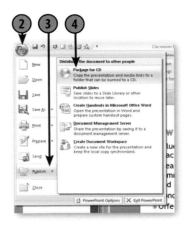

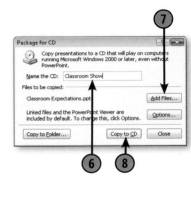

Tip ✓

The Options button in the Package for CD dialog box allows you to modify how presentations play in the PowerPoint Viewer and to choose whether to include linked files and TrueType fonts. If you want to be sure that the fonts in your presentation display accurately on another computer, be sure to select the Embedded TrueType Fonts option in the Options dialog box.

Tip ✓

If you'd rather publish your presentation to a location on your hard drive or other media, such as a flash drive, click Copy To Folder. You can then post the folder on the Web or access it from another computer on your network.

13

Running a Presentation

In this section:

- Starting and Ending a Slide Show
- Navigating through Slides
- Working with the Pen and Annotations

After you have built your slides, set up your slide show, rehearsed your presentation, and saved it to CD, the time comes to present your slide show to an audience. Assuming the show is set up to be given by a live presenter (see Section 12 for more about this setting) a presenter must know how to run the show, navigate among slides, annotate slides, and so on.

PowerPoint offers a few different ways to move around a presentation and a set of annotation tools that allows you to make notes as you present. If your presentation sparks interesting ideas, action items, or questions you need to follow up on, you can use the annotation tools to jot notes and save those annotations with your presentation. You can also switch to another program or even go online while presenting to display other kinds of documents and content.

Knowing how to use these tools can mean the difference between a smooth presentation and an awkward viewing and presenting experience.

Starting and Ending a Slide Show

Starting a slide show simply involves displaying the Slide Show view. This view shows your slides in full screen mode (unless you set up your show to be browsed by an individual, in which case your slides appear with a scrollbar around them). In Slide Show view, there are no speaker's notes or tool tabs in evidence, although there is a set of presentation tools that appear in the lower right corner of the screen when you move your mouse, which you learn more about in the following two tasks.

See Also

For information about navigating among views in PowerPoint, see "Running a Presentation in Slide Show View" on page 32.

See Also

To learn more about setting up your show to be browsed by individuals or run by a presenter, see "Setting Up a Slide Show" on page 178.

Start a Show

1. If you are using some form of LCD or other display equipment, connect it to your computer and turn it on.

2. Open the presentation you want to present.

3. If you want to start the show from the first slide, display it.

4. Click the Slide Show icon.

(continued on the next page)

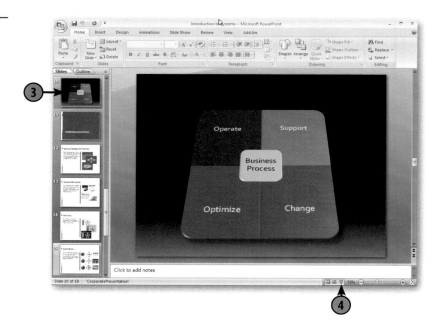

Start a Show *(continued)*

 The slide show begins.

 Tip

Always try to check the display equipment you are using before you present and, if possible, have the user manual for that equipment handy. In some cases you need to know which button or keystroke combinations to use to switch the display on or connect to your computer.

Tip

Another method you can use to start a slide show is to click the View tab on the ribbon in Normal or Slide Sorter view and then click the Slide Show button.

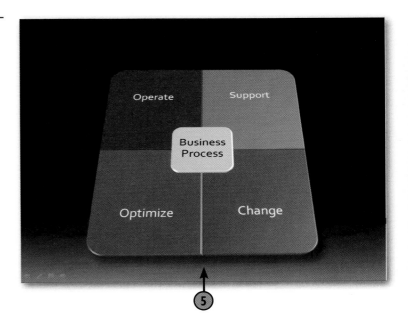

End a Show

1. With a presentation running in Slide Show mode, do one of the following:

   - Click Escape on your keyboard.
   - Click the Slide Show icon and choose End Show.
   - Press Ctrl+Break.
   - Press the hyphen key [-].
   - Navigate to the last slide in the presentation and press the right-arrow key on your keyboard. A black screen appears with a message that instructs you to click your mouse to end the show.

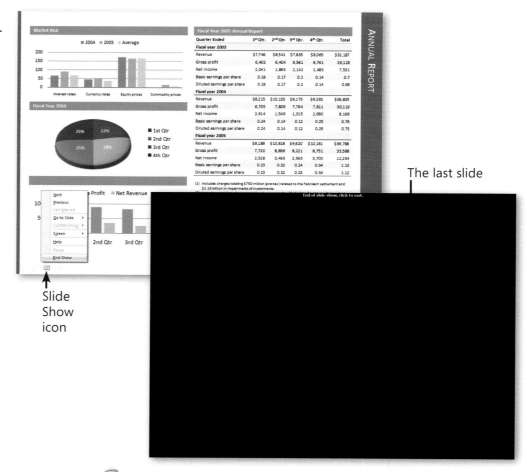

Slide
Show
icon

The last slide

Tip

If you want to temporarily remove your presentation from the screen, you don't have to exit the show. Instead, you can click the Slide Show icon and choose Screen and then the Black Screen or White Screen command. This is useful if you pause for a discussion and don't want people distracted by the words and images on screen.

Tip

Did you forget how to jump to another slide or some other handy navigation shortcut? Don't worry. Click the Slide Show icon and choose Help. A Slide Show Help window appears listing common keystroke commands. This list includes some very useful shortcuts; for example, to go to a black screen you can simply type "b".

Navigating through Slides

Many presenters begin at the first slide in their presentation and move to the last slide in order. But there are also times when you need to move back to a previous slide to reinforce a point or jump ahead when somebody anticipates a topic in a question or comment. For all of these scenarios you can use a few different methods to navigate from slide to slide.

Move to Next and Previous Slide

1 Click the Slide Show icon to display Slide Show view.

2 Use any of these methods to move to the next slide:

- Press the right arrow key on your keyboard.
- Click your mouse button.
- Click the Next arrow.
- Click the Slide Show icon and choose Next.
- Press the spacebar on your keyboard.

3 Use any of these methods to move to the previous slide:

- Press the left arrow key on your keyboard.
- Click the Previous arrow.
- Click the Slide Show icon and choose Previous.
- Press the Backspace key on your keyboard

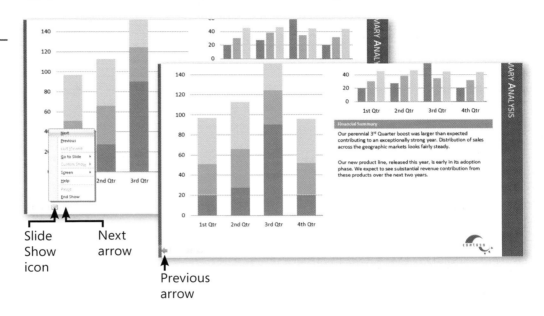

Slide Show icon

Next arrow

Previous arrow

Try This!

You can access the Slide Show menu by right-clicking anywhere on your screen while running a slide show. Then click Next or Previous to move forward or backward in your presentation.

Tip

Not enough options for you in this task to navigate from slide to slide? There are also two keystroke shortcuts you can use to move to the next or previous slide. Type "N" to go to the next slide, or "P" to go to the previous slide.

Go to a Particular Slide

1 Click the Slide Show icon to display Slide Show view.

2 Use any of these methods to move to any slide in the presentation:

- Click the Slide Show icon and choose Go To Slide, then click the title of the slide you want to go to.

- Type the slide number and press Enter.

- Press Ctrl+S. The All Slide dialog box appears showing a list of all slide titles. Click a title and then click Go to.

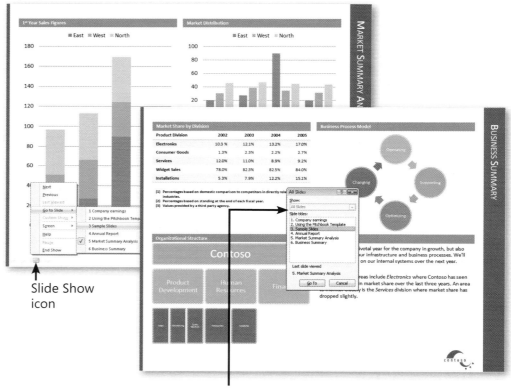

Slide Show icon

Press Ctrl+S to open the All Slide dialog box.

Tip

You can use the Home and End keys on your keyboard to move to the first or last slide in your presentation. You can also press and hold down both the right and left mouse buttons for a few seconds to jump to the last or first slide.

Try This!

You can decide you want to display a hidden slide. When you get to the slide before the hidden one, press "H" and Power-Point will go ahead and show the hidden slide. To return to the last slide you had displayed, click the Slide Show button and choose Last Viewed from the menu that appears.

Start a Custom Show

① Open a presentation that contains a custom show

② Click the Slide Show tab.

③ Click the Custom Slide Show button.

④ Click the custom show title.

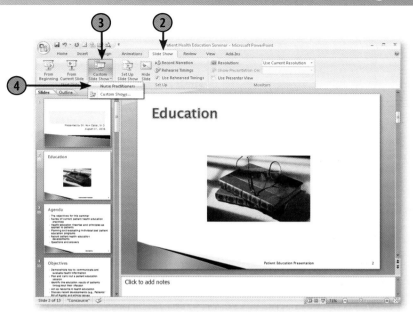

Try This!

If you create a large presentation, create summary slides that introduce each major section of the show. Then create a custom show that consists of those summary slides. You can then go to that custom show at the end of the larger show to review the major topics.

See Also

For information about working with custom shows, see "Creating a Custom Show" on page 217.

Working with the Pen and Annotations

A tool called a pen allows you to use a technology that Microsoft calls ink to write on your slides when running your show in Slide Show view. The Pen tool allows you to select different pen types, such as ballpoint, felt tip, and highlighter, and to change the ink color. You can use the pen to write on slides and then use an eraser tool to remove the writing, or use a command to remove all ink markings on a slide. At the end of your presentation you are offered the option of saving all your ink annotations or discarding them.

Choose a Pen Style and Color

1. Click the Slide Show view icon to begin your presentation.
2. Click the Pen button.
3. Click on a pen style to select it.
4. Click the Pen button again, and this time click Ink Color.
5. Click on a color in the pop-up palette that appears.

Try This!

You can also use the Pen menu to make changes to the cursor arrow that appears when the pen isn't activated. Click the Pen button and click Arrow to return to the arrow cursor after using the pen; open the menu again and click Arrow Options and choose Automatic, Visible, or Hidden to set whether the arrow pointer is visible only when you move the mouse or all the time, or if it will be invisible.

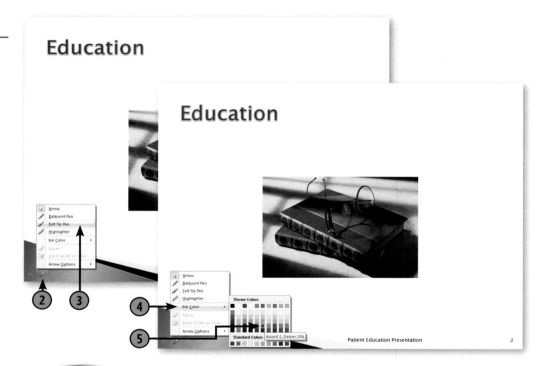

See Also

If you choose a pen color other than the default to write on a slide, be aware that when you move to another slide the default pen color takes over again. For more about choosing a default pen color, see "Specifying Show Options" on page 179.

Make Annotations on Slides

(1) With a slide displayed in Slide Show view, click the Pen button and choose a pen style.

(2) Click on your screen and draw or write wherever you wish, or if you chose the highlighter pen style, click and drag over the object or text you want to highlight.

(3) To turn off the pen, click the Pen button and choose Arrow.

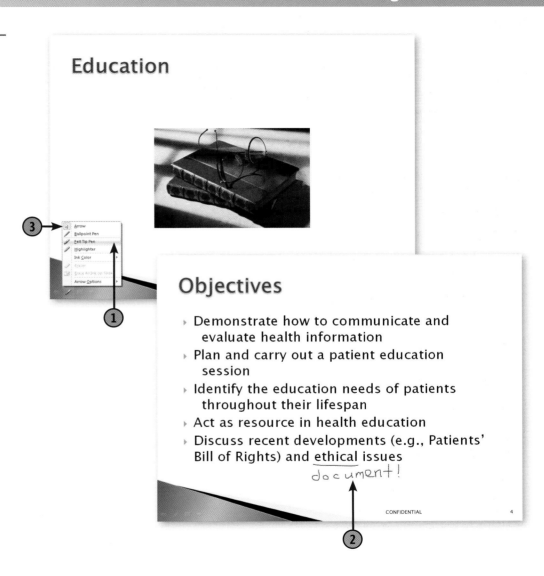

Erase Annotations on Slides

(1) Click the Pen icon.

(2) Choose Eraser.

(3) Move your cursor over the annotation you want to remove.

(4) To erase all annotations on a slide, click the Pen button and choose Erase All Ink On Slide.

Tip ✓

Here are a few shortcuts for turning these tools on and off. To quickly change from the arrow cursor to the Pen, press Ctrl+P. To change from the arrow cursor to the Eraser, press Ctrl+E. To turn off the Pen or Eraser tools, you can simply press Escape on your keyboard.

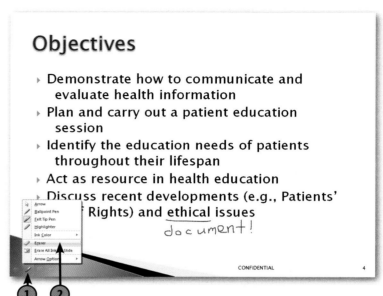

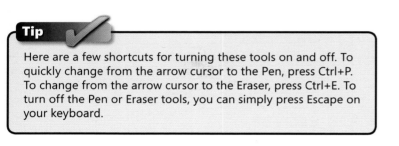

Save Annotations

① Navigate to the end of a presentation in which you've made annotations.

② When you click to end the show, a dialog box appears.

③ Click Keep to save your annotations and Discard if you don't want to save them.

④ Saved annotations appear on the slide in Normal view.

Tip

Note that after you save an annotation, even if you go back into Slide Show view, you can't use the Eraser tool to erase it. That's because ink annotations are objects that can be resized, rotated, moved, and so on, just like any other object. To remove them from your presentation in Normal view, you can simply click on them and press Delete.

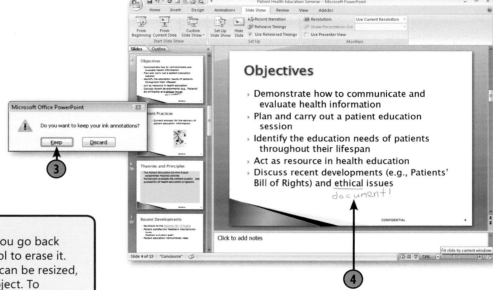

Switching to Another Program

There are many reasons for switching to another program while running a PowerPoint presentation. You might want to demo a software system or run a new product demo in a movie program, or you may want to go onto the Internet and browse for information to answer a question. Although you can place links in your presentation that open documents in other programs, if you prefer to open the programs themselves to work in them, you can do so easily.

Switch to Another Program

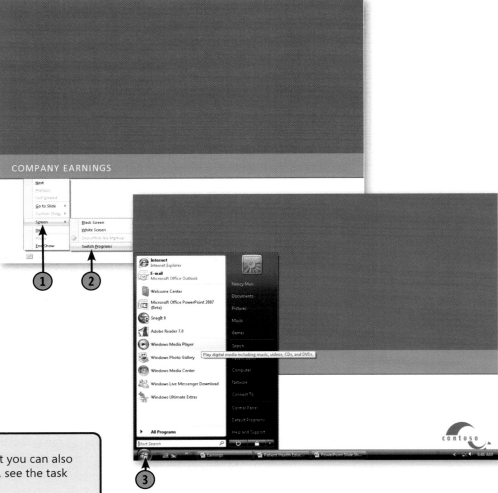

(1) With a slide show running, click the Slide Show button and choose Screen.

(2) Click Switch Programs.

(3) Click the Start button on the Windows taskbar that appears and choose All Programs, and then click the program you want to run.

(4) When you're done working in the program simply click the Close button and click anywhere on your slide show screen to remove the taskbar.

Tip

To save time, you might open the other programs you want to use before you start your show. Then, when you display the Windows taskbar, you can simply click on the minimized program on the taskbar to open it.

See Also

For more information about action buttons that you can also use to jump to other documents and programs, see the task "Drawing Shapes and Text Boxes" on page 120.

14

Printing a Presentation

In this section:

- **Inserting Headers and Footers**
- **Using Print Preview**
- **Establishing Printer Settings and Printing Options**

You may choose to print your presentation for any number of reasons. Perhaps you want others to review it to help you correct or edit it before you present your slide show. You may also want to print audience handouts or a copy for yourself to refer to while presenting the show. You might want to preserve a printout of the outline of your contents for your files or to use as the basis of another document.

Whatever your reason for printing your presentation, PowerPoint provides tools to help you preview your printed document, add headers or footers, and choose various printing options such as page orientation.

When you print your slides, you can choose how many slides to fit to a page. You can print audience handouts that place several slides on a page and leave space for taking notes. You can also print one slide per page with your speaker notes included. Finally, you can print the Outline view, which includes only the outline text.

Inserting Headers and Footers

When you print slides you may want to include information such as slide number, the date and time the presentation is printed, or the name of the author of the presentation. To do so, you use the Header and Footer feature. You can insert separate headers and footers on slides and on notes and handouts. You can also choose to omit header and footer text on the title slide of the presentation.

See Also

For information about using footer placeholders using the slide master feature, see "Insert Footer Information" on page 146.

Tip

In addition to using the Insert menu command, you can change header and footer settings from Print Preview by clicking Options, Header and Footer.

Insert Headers or Footers

① Click the Insert tab.

② Click Header & Footer.

(continued on the next page)

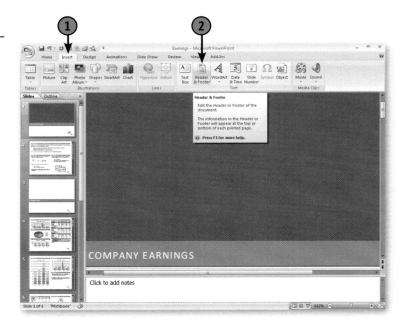

Insert Headers or Footers *(continued)*

(3) Click either the Slide or Notes And Handouts tab, depending on where you want to set headers and footers.

(4) Click the Date And Time check box to include a date and/or time and choose either of these options:

■ Update Automatically, to include the current date and/or time. If you choose this option, use the drop down lists to select a date/time format, language, and calendar type. The date will update every time you open the slide show.

■ Fixed, to include a date you specify by typing it in.

(5) Click the Slide Number check box to include the number of each slide.

(6) Click the Footer check box and enter text to appear in a footer.

(7) If you are on the Slide tab, you can also check the Don't Show On Title Slide check box to omit the footer information from any slide with a Title Slide layout.

(8) Click Apply To All to apply the settings to all slides. On the Slide tab you have the option to click Apply if you want to apply the settings only to the current slide.

(9) Placeholders now appear on slides.

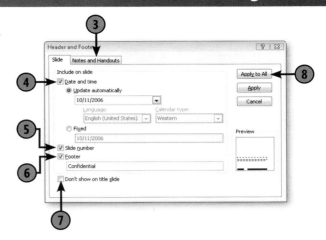

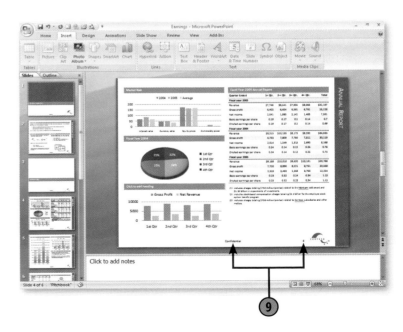

Tip

Note that all items inserted using the Slide tab of the Header and Footer dialog box are inserted as footers, but you can click and drag footers to place them anywhere on an individual slide in Normal view. Notes and Handouts use both header and footer placeholders, and again, you can move those placeholders around in the Notes Page view or Handout Master.

Using Print Preview

PowerPoint never had a print preview feature before because you could see how slides would appear by running a slide show. But in PowerPoint 2007, Print Preview has been added, and it's very useful for viewing previews of printed documents including handouts, Outline view, and notes pages before you print them. Print Preview also offers several tools for setting the page orientation and various other printing options from one location.

Display Print Preview

1. Click the Office button.
2. Click Print.
3. Click Print Preview.
4. Click to select the format of output you want to preview in the Print What drop-down list.

Tip

The Zoom slider feature in the bottom right corner of the PowerPoint window works in Print Preview as well. Use it to zoom in and out of your preview to review the contents.

See Also

You can add a Print Preview icon to the Quick Access toolbar if you want to be able to go to Print Preview with a single click. For more information about setting up the Quick Access toolbar, see "Customize the Quick Access Toolbar" on page 14.

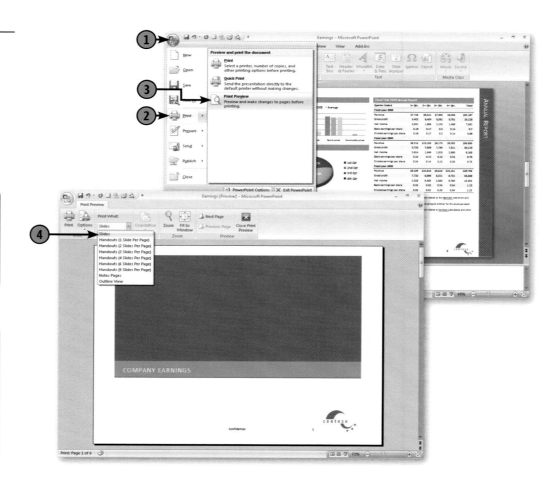

Navigate the Print Preview

1. Click and drag the scrollbar to move to any other slide in the presentation.

2. Click under or above the scrollbar to move forward or backward one slide or page at a time.

3. Click the Next Page or Previous Page button to move forward or backward one slide or page at a time.

4. Click Fit To Window to adjust the size of the slide to fill the window.

5. Click Close Print Preview to leave the Print Preview without printing, or...

6. Click Print to print the document.

Tip

You can click the Options button in Print Preview to set printing options such as using color or grayscale, scaling the printed output to fit the specified paper, adding a frame to slides, printing hidden slides or comments, and specifying the print order for pages.

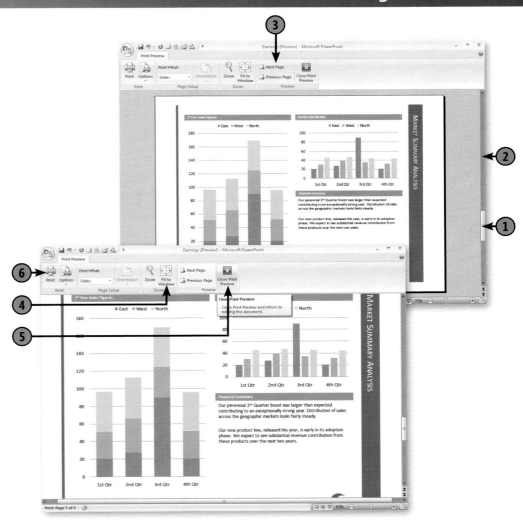

Establishing Printer Settings and Printing

The PowerPoint Print dialog box contains some settings that are probably familiar to you from other programs, such as word processors or spreadsheet programs, and some that are very specific to PowerPoint. For example, you can choose to print slides, the presentation outline, handouts, or notes pages. You can also choose how many slides to include on a single page if you are printing slides, handouts, or notes.

Choose a Printer and Paper Options

1 Click the Office button.

2 Click Print.

3 Click Print.

(continued on the next page)

Tip

If you want the same printer to be the default option every time you print, you can go to the Windows Control Panel (Start, Control Panel, and click the Printer link), right-click a printer, and choose Set As Default Printer. You can still change the printer choice in a Print dialog box, but the new setting will only apply to the document you are printing.

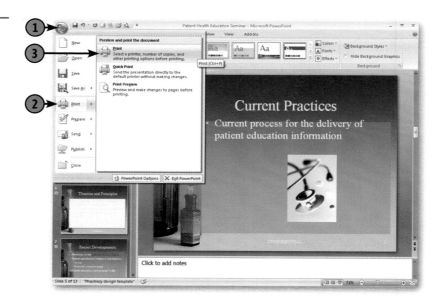

Choose a Printer and Paper Options *(continued)*

④ Click and choose a printer from the Name drop-down list.

⑤ Click the Properties button. (Note that your Properties dialog box shows settings specific to your printer model).

⑥ Click to select the paper size.

⑦ Click to select the page orientation.

⑧ Click OK to save the setting and return to the Print dialog box. At this point, you can continue to change the settings as described in the next three tasks or click Print to print your presentation.

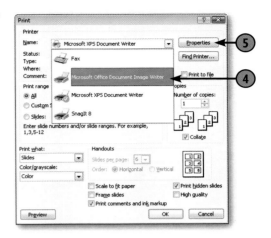

Tip ✓

Different printers may offer different property options. For example, if you have a color printer you can choose to print in color or grayscale. You may be able to select media type, such as printing to glossy paper or to transparencies for overhead projection. Take a look at your Printer Properties dialog box to see what other settings might be available to you.

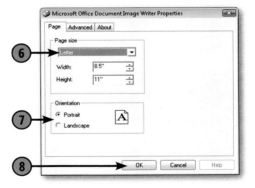

Choose Which Slides to Print

① Open the Print dialog box (see previous task).

② Choose any of the following options:

- Click All to print all the slides in the presentation.

- Click Current Slide to print only the currently displayed slide.

- Click Selection to print whatever contents you selected prior to opening the Print dialog box.

- Click Slides and enter slide numbers or a range (2, 15, or 3–15, for example) to print a range or selection of slides.

③ Click OK to print the specified slides.

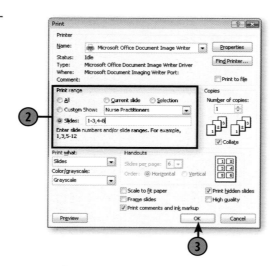

Tip

It's easiest to use the Slide Sorter view to select certain slides prior to using the Selection option in the Print dialog box. Display this view and click on one slide, then hold down the Ctrl key on your keyboard and click other slides to include. Then go to the Print dialog box and print your selection.

See Also

For more information about displaying the Slide Sorter view, see "Display Slide Sorter View" on page 31.

Choose the Format to Print

① Open the Print dialog box.

② Click the Print What field and choose the type of output to print.

③ If you selected Handouts or Notes in Step 2, click the Slides Per Page field and select the number of slides to include on each page of printed output.

④ Click Horizontal to have pages with multiple slides progress from right to left across the page; click Vertical to have slides progress down the page along the left and then move to the top of the right side of the page for the second column.

⑤ Click OK to print.

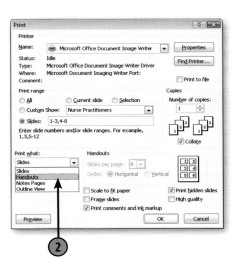

Tip

If you want to prepare a printed document in Word rather than PowerPoint, you can use the Publish command under the Power-Point Office button menu to send your presentation to Microsoft Word and prepare handout pages or an outline for printing. You can then simply print from Word's Print dialog box.

See Also

For more information about working with handouts and notes layouts, see "Working with Handout and Notes Masters" on page 152.

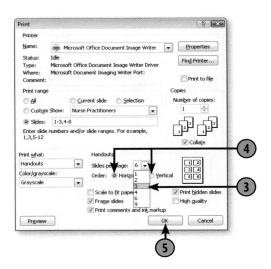

Specify the Number of Copies and Print

(1) Click the Office button.

(2) Click Print.

(3) Click Print.

(4) Click the spinner arrows up or down on the Number Of Copies field until the number of copies you want to print appears there.

(5) Click the Collate check box to collate the pages of multiple copies.

(6) Click OK to print.

Tip

If you have to print a lot of copies and want to save pages, consider modifying the number of slides per page that you print for handouts or notes pages. For more information about this setting, see the task "Choose the Format to Print" in this section.

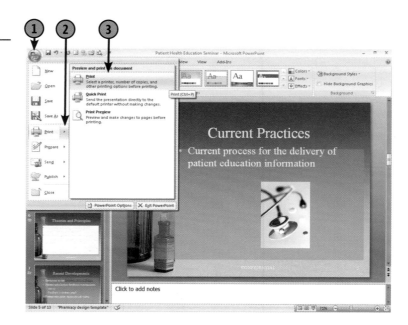

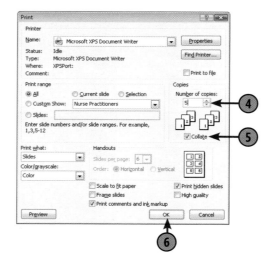

Publishing a Presentation to the Web

In this section:

- Saving a Presentation as a Web Page
- Publishing a Presentation to the Web

The ability to publish a presentation to the Internet as a Web document allows you to share your ideas with anybody, any time. You could, for example, publish your presentation as a follow up to giving it in person, so your audience can review or print out the content for themselves, at their leisure. You might also publish a presentation to the Web for others to review and suggest changes before you present it.

You can save a presentation in a couple of Web page formats. Web Page saves all the files of your presentation in a single folder for publishing on the Web. Single File Web Page saves your file in a multi-lingual hypertext markup language (MHTML) format that provides your Web page contents in a single file, which is somewhat smaller than the folder version and can be easier to manage if you email your site contents to others.

Finally, you can modify various Web options that allow you to include navigation tools, resize graphics for browser windows, and apply settings for fonts and other elements of the presentation to optimize it for the Web. For example, you can specify whether navigation controls should be included so that those viewing the page can easily move from slide to slide, which browsers are most likely to be used to view the presentation, and how fonts are managed when your slides are viewed online.

Saving a Presentation as a Web Page

When you save a presentation as a Web Page, you save an .htm file along with various files required for your Web page, such as the graphic images, sounds, styles, and so on. If you want to edit your Web site with some other program such as FrontPage, the Web Page format is your best bet. If you choose to save as a Single File Web Page, you save a single file that includes all the elements of your presentation; this presentation is easier to share but not editable.

Tip

If you have access to a SharePoint site online, you might also explore publishing your presentation in a document workspace in the PowerPoint Help system. This allows easy sharing with others who have access to your site.

Tip

Previous versions of PowerPoint contained a Web toolbar, but that feature is gone in 2007. Instead, you can add Web tools to the Quick Access toolbar (see Section 2 for more about this toolbar). The tools you can place here include the Web Options button and Web Page Preview button.

Choose a Web Page Format

1 Click the Office button.

2 Click Save As.

3 Click Other Formats.

(continued on the next page)

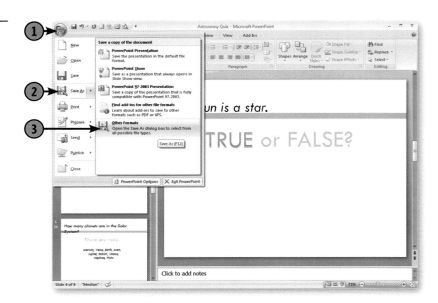

Choose a Web Page Format *(continued)*

④ Click the arrow in the Save As Type field to open the list.

⑤ Choose either Web Page or Single File Web Page.

⑥ Click the Change Title button.

⑦ Enter the page title you want to appear in the title bar of the viewer's browser.

⑧ Click OK.

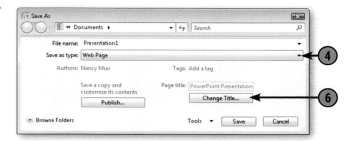

You can add a word or words that help identify the file by clicking in the Add A Tag field in the Save As dialog box. These act as keywords you can use to locate the file. If you add a tag to a file and then click the Office button, Prepare, and finally Properties, you will see any tags you added listed as keywords on the Summary tab.

Set up Web Options

1. With the Save As dialog box open click Tools.

2. Click Web Options.

3. Click the various tabs to change the following settings:

   ■ **General tab.** Here you indicate that you want to include navigation controls, to show animations when somebody is browsing your presentation, or to resize graphics to fit the viewer's browser window.

   ■ **Browsers tab.** Here you can select the browser most people are likely to use to view your presentation, and various options for dealing with graphics and Web page formats.

   ■ **Files tab.** Here you set can control how Web files are organized and which is the default editor for Web pages you create in Office.

   ■ **Pictures tab.** Set the screen resolution for your presentation here.

   ■ **Encoding tab.** You can choose different character sets, such as Western European, ASCII, or Japanese to save presentations in.

   ■ **Fonts tab.** Choose the default fonts for your presentation here.

4. Click OK to save the settings.

5. Click Save to save the Web file with the settings you've made.

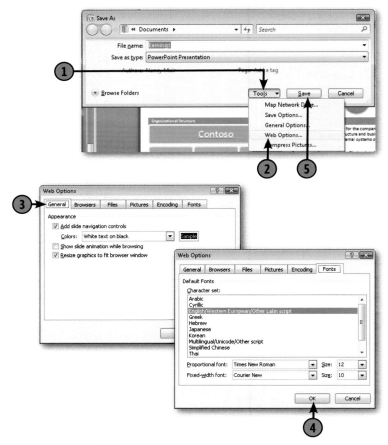

See Also

For information about saving your presentation to the default PowerPoint format, see "Save a Presentation" on page 34.

Tip

This task saves a file or set of files to your hard drive or storage media in a Web page format; to publish the presentation to the Web see the next task, "Publishing a Presentation as a Web Page."

Publishing a Presentation as a Web Page

When you publish a presentation to the Web you actually specify a location on your intranet or on the Internet to save the file to where others can access it. PowerPoint allows you to make several settings when you publish a presentation, including choosing which slides to publish and which browsers you think most of your viewers will use to run the presentation.

Choose Browser Support

1. With the Publish as Web Page dialog box open (see next task, steps 1 through 5) choose one of the following:

   - Microsoft Internet Explorer 4.0 Or Later if most people viewing your presentation are using this version of Internet Explorer only.

   - Microsoft Internet Explorer 3.0, Netscape Navigator 3.0, Or Later if you expect a mix of people using the two most popular browsers to view your presentation.

   - Selecting All Browsers Listed Above creates a larger file, but this is the best choice if you're not really sure which browsers your viewers will be using.

2. Click Publish to publish the file. If you have clicked the Open Published Web Page In Browser check box, a preview appears.

3. Click the Close button in your browser to close the preview.

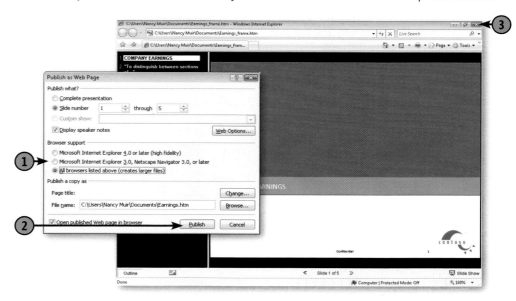

Tip

If your browser is set up to block ActiveX scripts, you may not have full access to various navigation tools in the Web page preview. Disable this setting or if a message appears that allows you to make choices about blocking these scripts, click on it and choose to allow blocked scripts.

Try This!

If you preview your Web page, use the navigation tools along the bottom of the browser window to expand the presentation outline, or move from slide to slide. If you want to go into full screen slide show mode, click the Slide Show button in the lower right corner. Press Escape to close the full screen mode.

Choose Which Slides to Publish

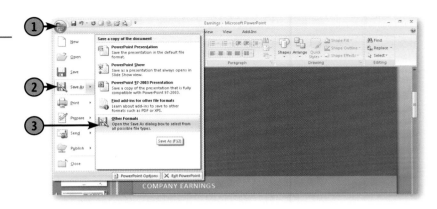

(1) Click the Office button.

(2) Click Save As.

(3) Click Other Formats.

(4) Click the Save As Type field and choose Web Page or Single File Web Page.

(5) Click Publish.

(6) Click an option to specify what to publish:

- Select Complete Presentation to publish all slides.

- Select Slide Number and enter a beginning and ending slide number to select a subset of slides to publish.

- Select Display Speaker Notes if you want to include notes with the slides you publish.

(7) Enter a location to publish the file to in the File Name field.

(8) Click Publish. If you have clicked the Open Published Web Page In Browser check box, a preview appears.

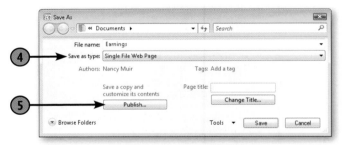

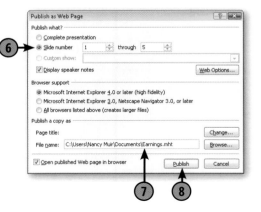

Try This!

Create a custom show within your presentation and then you can click Custom Show and choose the custom show to use. This allows you to publish a show that picks and chooses various slides in your presentation, rather than a range of slides.

Tip

If you want to preview the presentation as a Web page, click Open Published Web Page In Browser at the bottom of the Publish as Web Page dialog box.

16 Introducing Advanced Power-Point Topics

In this section:

- **Saving Your Own PowerPoint Templates**
- **Creating Custom Shows**
- **Removing Hidden Data with Document Inspector**
- **Adding a Digital Signature to a Presentation**

The preceding sections of this book cover the topics you need to create most presentations and to use PowerPoint efficiently. However, there are some more advanced features that you may want to explore in this section that help you work more efficiently.

You can develop a presentation that forms the basis of other presentations and save that presentation as a template. This can save you a great deal of work in setting up themes, layouts, and slide master settings for each new presentation.

Custom shows are subsets of the slides in a presentation that can be saved right inside the same file. Custom shows may contain only some of the slides of the presentation or rearrange the order of slides. For example, if you have a master presentation on your entire product line, you can save custom shows that focus on each product line separately and show only the presentation that relates to an individual customer's needs.

A new feature called Document Inspector allows you to search your files for hidden data and remove it before saving the file. Finally, you can add a digital signature to your presentation. A digital signature assures whoever opens the file that it came from you.

Saving Your Own PowerPoint Templates

You can save any file in a template format (.potx). A template can contain various custom settings, such as changes you make to the slide master, custom layouts or animations you created, or themes and font choices you applied. Your templates can also contain text or graphic elements in placeholders. By using a template as the basis of a new presentation, you can not only save time but guarantee a consistency of look and feel among all your presentations.

Tip

Remember, after you open a template, you need to save it as a regular PowerPoint presentation with a new name so you don't overwrite the template with presentation-specific changes. For more information about saving files, see "Saving and Closing a PowerPoint Presentation" on page 34.

Tip

If you have access to a SharePoint site or a company intranet, you might consider sharing templates across an organization so all presentations have a consistent company look and feel.

Save a Presentation as a Template

① Make any settings or changes you wish to the presentation, and then click the Office button.

② Click Save As.

③ Click Other Formats.

(continued on the next page)

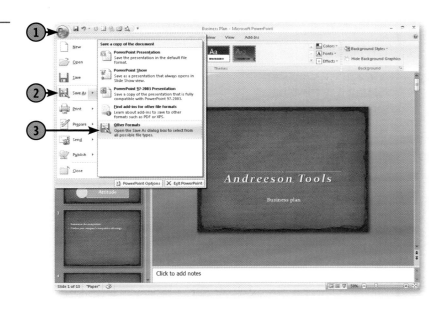

Save a Presentation as a Template *(continued)*

④ Click the Save As Type field and choose PowerPoint Template.

⑤ Enter a name in the File Name field.

⑥ Click Save.

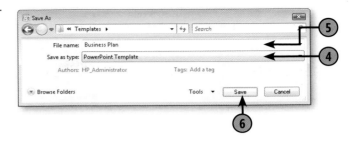

Tip

If you or somebody else wants to use the template with an earlier version of PowerPoint, you should choose PowerPoint 97-2003 Template in Step 4. This is useful if you are sharing a template with people working on earlier versions of the software.

Creating a Custom Show

The ability to create and store custom shows within a single presentation file offers you great flexibility. You can create several custom shows from one presentation by simply choosing the slides to include and reorganizing them in any way you wish. The slides in a custom show remain identical to the corresponding slides in your main presentation, but by selecting and rearranging their order, you can create quite different shows to meet your viewers' needs.

Create a Custom Show

① Click the Slide Show tab.

② Click Custom Slide Show.

③ Click Custom Shows.

④ Click New.

⑤ Click a slide in the Slides In Presentation list.

⑥ Click Add. Repeat steps 5 and 6 to add all the slides you want in your custom show.

⑦ Click a slide in the Slides In Custom Show list.

⑧ Use the Move Up and Move Down buttons to reorganize the slide order. Repeat these steps with other slides until your slides are in the order you want.

⑨ Enter a name in the Slide Show Name field.

⑩ Click OK.

⑪ Click Close to close the Custom Shows dialog box.

Tip

If you change your mind about including a slide in a custom show, click that slide in the Slides In Custom Show list and click the Remove button.

Try This!

If you have created a custom show and then need to edit it, click the Custom Slide Show button on the Slide Show tab. Click on the show and then click the Edit button. Use the steps outlined above to add, remove, or rearrange the slides in the show, then click OK.

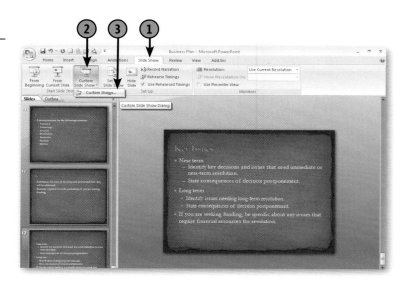

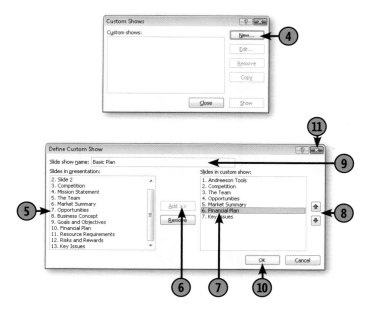

Run a Custom Show

1 Click the Slide Show tab.

2 Click Custom Slide Show.

3 Click the name of the custom show. The show begins to run.

4 Use the navigation tools to move through the presentation. Press Escape to stop the show at any time.

Tip

You can use the Set Up Show dialog box (click the Set Up Slide Show button on the Slide Show tab) to set up your file to play a custom show whenever you click the Slide Show button. Just select the custom show you want to use from the Custom Show field.

See Also

For more information about using navigation tools in Slide Show view, see "Navigating through Slides" on page 191.

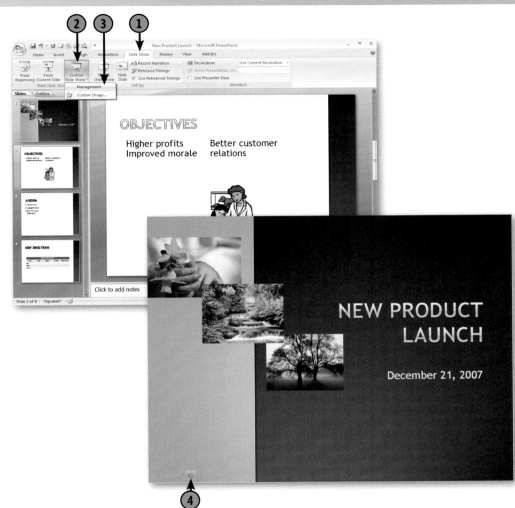

Removing Hidden Data with Document Inspector

When you intend to share a presentation either by publishing it online or by handing it to somebody on a CD, it's a good idea to make sure there isn't any hidden data included. For example, a file may contain personal information about the author or document properties, called metadata, that you'd rather not share. You can use the new Document Inspector feature of PowerPoint to remove such information.

Remove Hidden Data with Document Inspector

① Save a copy of your presentation with a new name.

② Click the Office button.

③ Click Prepare.

④ Click Inspect Document.

⑤ Click various check boxes to choose what content to inspect for.

⑥ Click Inspect.

(continued on the next page)

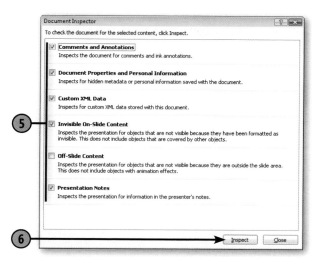

Remove Hidden Data with Document
Inspector *(continued)*

⑦ Click any Remove All buttons that appear in the results window.

⑧ Click Close to save the file with the selected data omitted.

Tip

I start out this task by having you save a copy of the presentation because much of the data you delete using Document Inspector cannot be restored. The data that Document Inspector removes might be useful information for a presentation you are still working on, such as the date you last made a change to the presentation or invisible contents on slides. Working on a copy saves that data on the original.

Try This!

If you want to manually edit your presentation properties to remove personal information instead of letting Document Inspector do all the work, click the Office button, choose Prepare, and then click on Properties. Just delete any data in any field that you don't want included with the file.

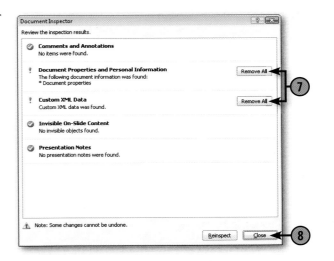

Adding a Digital Signature

A digital signature is much like a handwritten signature on a check or other legal document. It can be used to ensure that the document was created by a particular person. In a world where computer files can contain potentially harmful materials, a digital signature helps to reassure a recipient that the file was created by somebody they know and trust. You can use a digital signature provided by a third party that others can use to verify your document. You can also create one that only serves for you to verify that a document you open on your computer is your own.

Purchase a Third-Party Digital Signature Product

① Be sure your computer is connected to the Internet and then click the Office button.

② Click Prepare.

③ Click Add a Digital Signature.

④ In the confirming dialog box that appears, click Signature Services From The Office Marketplace.

(continued on the next page)

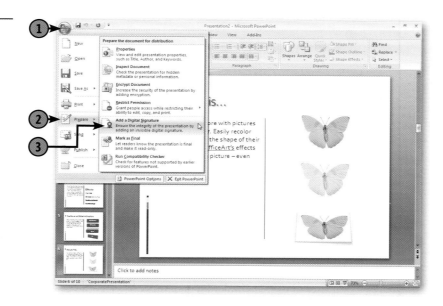

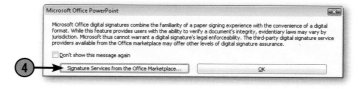

Purchase a Third-Party Digital Signature Product *(continued)*

⑤ Click on a digital signing provider in the list.

⑥ Click the Try [service name] button and follow the steps to purchase a digital signature product or download a free trial.

Digital Signing software can cost anywhere from under $100 to over $250. You might make this investment if it's important that you be sure that documents come from the person they purport to be from, and that the contents of the document haven't been changed since they were signed.

Try This!

You can also use the Information Rights Management Service to authenticate the sender and recipient of files sent by e-mail to ensure that your files don't fall into the wrong hands. Click the Review tab and then click the Protect Presentation button and choose Restricted Access. Follow the instructions to sign up for this service from Microsoft.

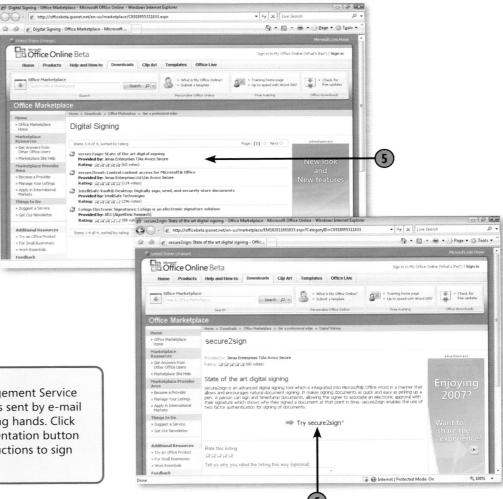

Create Your Own Digital Signature

(1) Save your file as a PowerPoint presentation and click the Office button.

(2) Click Prepare.

(3) Click Add a Digital Signature.

(4) In the confirming dialog box that appears, click OK to proceed. If you have saved a digital signature before, skip to step 9.

(5) Click Create Your Own Digital ID.

(6) Click OK.

(7) Enter your name, e-mail address, organization, and location in the Create a Digital ID dialog box.

(8) Click Create.

(continued on the next page)

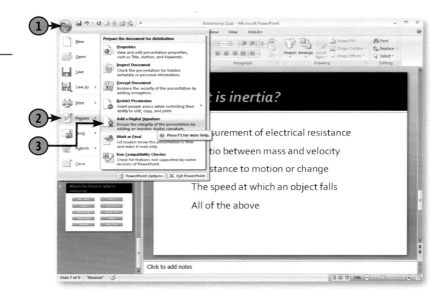

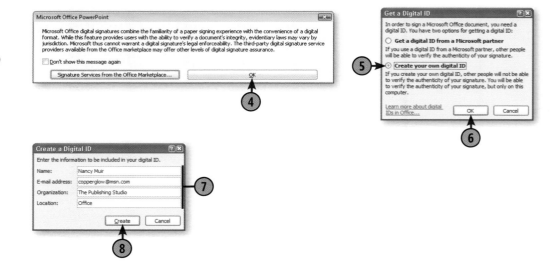

Create Your Own Digital Signature *(continued)*

(9) In the Sign dialog box, fill in the Purpose For Signing This Document field.

(10) Click Sign.

(11) In the Signature Confirmation dialog box click OK.

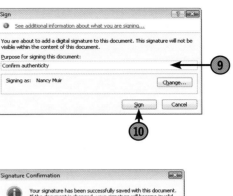

Tip

To view signatures associated with a document, click the Office button, click Prepare, and then click View Signatures. A Signatures pane appears listing any signatures associated with the file. Click on a signature listed there to view its details.

Index

3-D rotation effects, 135

A

action buttons, 121
Action Settings dialog box, 121
actions
  passing mouse over object, 121
  undoing and redoing, 44
  when clicking on object, 121
ActiveX scripts, 213
add-in programs, 9
Add-ins tab, 8
All Borders style, 93
All Slide dialog box, 192
alternative words for text, 174–75
animations, 122
  custom, 165
  delay between, 166
  deleting, 167
  modifying settings, 166–67
  motion path, 157
  multiple, 168
  Normal view, 159
  playing in sequence, 169
  previewing, 169
  reordering effects, 168
  timing, 169
annotations
  adding, 195
  running slide show, 179
  saving, 197
  slide shows, 33
Apply To All Slides command, 81, 84
Apply To Selected Slides command, 81, 84

Arrange, Align, Align To Slide
  command, 94

B

background
  changing, 141
  customizing, 141
  handouts, 153, 155
  styles, 141
Background gallery, 141
Backspace key, 43, 191
Black Screen command, 190
blank presentations, 24
blank slides, 39
blank templates, 24
blocking ActiveX scripts, 213
Border tool, 92
brightness, 139
browsers, 212–13
bulleted points, 38
  automatically entering, 40
  modifying styles, 40
  slide layouts, 77

C

Change Chart Type dialog box, 97
Change to Eraser (Ctrl+E) keyboard
  shortcut, 196
Change to Pen Tool (Ctrl+P) keyboard
  shortcut, 196
character spacing, 129
Chart Layout gallery, 98

Chart Styles gallery, 98
charts
  changing style and layout, 98–99
  displaying or hiding legend, 100–01
  formatting legend, 101
  inserting, 96–97
  manually modifying, 99
  masters, 147
  source data, 97
  styles, 96, 99
  types, 97
checking spelling. *See* spell checking
Choose a SmartArt Graphic dialog box,
  22, 110
Choose Theme or Themed Document
  dialog box, 83
clip art
  dragging and dropping, 104
  fills, 131
  finding, 102–03
  inserting, 104–05
  masters, 147
  permissions, 102
  viewing collections on Microsoft Office
    Web site, 103
Clip Art icon, 102
Clip Art task pane, 103–05, 116
Color dialog box, 127
color schemes, 73, 84
colors
  RGB (Red/Green/Blue) color system, 127
  text, 126–27
  themes, 21
Colors dialog box, 179
commands and keyboard shortcuts, 24
comments, 176

Comparison slide layout, 39, 89
content placeholder, 38, 40, 112
content slide, 38
contextual toolbar, 127
contextual tools, 3
contrast, 139
Copy (Ctrl+C) keyboard shortcut, 68
copying
    and pasting slides, 68
    text, 44
Create Chart dialog box, 96
Create Handouts in Microsoft Office Word
        option, 62
Crop tool, 134
cropping pictures, 114–15, 134
cropping tool, 115
custom animation, 165
Custom Animation task pane, 166
    Amount field, 167
    AutoPreview check box, 169
    Font Size field, 167
    Move Down button, 168
    Move Up button, 168
    Remove button, 167
    Slide Show button, 169
    Speed field, 167
    Start field, 167
Custom Layout slide, 148
custom slide shows, 193, 214–16
    creation, 217
    running, 219
custom themes and SharePoint
        sites, 150
Customize window, 16
customizing
    background, 141
    character spacing, 129
    Quick Access toolbar, 14–17
    themes, 85

Cut (Ctrl+X) keyboard shortcut, 68
cutting text, 44

D

data, removing hidden, 220–21
Date and Time dialog box, 42
dates
    automatically reflecting, 146
    footers, 146
    headers and footers, 201
    notes, 154
    slides, 42
Delete Slide command, 67
Demote (Tab) keyboard shortcut, 57
design elements
    color schemes, 73
    previewing, 18–19
    slide layouts, 73
    SmartArt, 22
    themes, 20–21, 73
diagrams, 109
Dialog Box Launcher, 9
dialog boxes, opening, 9
digital signatures
    third-party, 222–23
    user-created, 224–25
    viewing, 225
Digital Signing software, 223
display equipment, 189
Document Inspector, 215, 220–21
Draw Table tool, 92
duplicating
    placeholders, 44, 78
    slides, 69

E

e-mailing presentations for review, 177
Edit Photo Album dialog box, 119
editing text, 43
effects
    objects, 130–31
    reordering, 168
    shapes, 133
e-mailing presentations attached as
        PowerPoint files, 177
End Show (Ctrl+Break) keyboard
        shortcut, 190
ending slide shows, 190
erasing annotations on slides, 196
Esc key, 190
expanding and collapsing outlines, 58–59

F

features
    customizing Quick Access toolbar,
        14–17
    design elements, 17–22
    including, 9
    Mini toolbar, 12–13
    Quick Access toolbar, 6
    ribbon, 5–6
    ScreenTips, 10–11
File, Close command, 35
File, New command, 24
File, Open command, 27
File, PowerPoint Options command, 10, 12
File, Save As, Other Format command, 34
File, Save command, 34
File, Save As command, 34
File menu, 3, 5
    accessing, 7

File menu, *continued*
  recently used files, 27
files
  finding, 27
  overwriting original, 25
  recently used, 27
  renaming, 25
fill color, 51, 130–31
finalizing presentations, 171
Find and Replace dialog box, 47
finding
  clip art, 102–03
  files, 27
  and replacing text, 45–46
  themes online, 82–83
First Slide (Home) keyboard shortcut, 192
Fit Slide to Current Window button, 29
flipping objects, 136
Font dialog box, 125, 129
font sets, 41
font sizes
  outlines, 55
  previewing, 19
fonts, 19
  changing, 125
  default, 212
  difficulty reading, 128
  notes, 155
  preinstalled, 124
  presentations, 185
  previewing, 85, 125
  selecting, 124–25
  symbols, 41
  themes, 85
Fonts gallery, 85
Footer placeholder, 148
footers
  date and time, 42
  inserting information on master, 146
  placeholders, 146

footers, *continued*
  returning placeholders to default, 146
  slide number element, 146
Format Background dialog box, 141
Format Legend command, 101
Format Legend dialog box, 101
Format Shape command, 51, 122
Format Shape dialog box, 122, 133, 139
formatting
  handouts, 153
  notes, 155
  objects, 130–33
  placeholders, 51
  text, 12–13, 55, 61, 126–29
  text boxes, 122
  turning on and off in outlines, 61

G

galleries, 5, 17–19
graphics, 87
  galleries, 5, 17
  handouts, 153
  masters, 147
  omitting from individual slides, 149
  overlapping placeholders, 147
  slide layouts, 77
  Web pages, 212
grouping objects, 123, 136–37

H

Handout master, 143, 152–53
handouts, 152
  background, 153, 155
  formatting, 153
  graphics, 153
  placeholders, 153

handouts, *continued*
  portrait or landscape orientation, 153
  slides per page, 153
Header and Footer dialog box, 201
Header and Footer feature, 200–01
headers and footers, 200–01
headings, promoting and demoting, 57
help, 36
Hidden Slide (H) keyboard shortcut, 192
hidden slides, displaying, 192
hiding and unhiding slides, 70–71
hyperlinks, pasting as, 44
hyphen key (-), 190

I

images, organizing, 113
indented bullets levels, 57
Information Rights Management
  Service, 223
Insert Picture dialog box, 110

K

kerning, 129
keyboard and advancing slides, 164
keyboard shortcuts, 190
  commands and, 24
  for tool button functions, 11

L

Last Slide (End) keyboard shortcut, 192
Last Viewed command, 192
Layout gallery, 76
left arrow key, 191
Live Preview feature, 131
looping slide shows, 178–79

M

Master Layout thumbnail, 148
masters, 81, 123, 143
    adding, 152
    adding layout to, 148
    automatically adding themes, 152
    charts, 147
    clip art, 147
    Custom Layout slide, 148
    deleting, 151
    displaying, 145
    graphics, 147
    inserting footer information, 146
    making changes to, 144
    modifying, 145
    navigating, 145
    omitting graphics from individual
        slides, 149
    pictures, 147
    placeholders, 148
    renaming, 150
microphone, 182–83
Microphone Check dialog box, 183
Microsoft Internet Explorer, 213
Microsoft Office PowerPoint
    closing, 35
Microsoft Office PowerPoint window, 36
Microsoft Office Web site, viewing clip art
    collections, 103
Microsoft Office Word
    printing slides, 207
    sending outline to, 62–63
Microsoft Typography Web site, 124
Mini toolbar, 12–13, 43, 57
minimized programs, 198
motion path, 157
Move Down command, 60, 70
Move Up command, 60, 70

movies, 116–17
moving slides, 70
multi-lingual hypertext markup format
    (MHTML), 209
multimedia clips, automatically
    playing, 117
multimedia objects, 116–17

N

narration
    recording, 181, 182–83
    setting microphone level, 182
navigating
    Print Preview, 203
    slides, 191–93
Netscape Navigator, 213
New Presentation (Ctrl+N) keyboard
    shortcut, 24
New Presentation window, 24–26
Next command, 191
Next Slide (N) keyboard shortcut, 191
Normal view, 28, 48, 53
    applied transitions or animation, 159
    applying themes, 152
    entering text, 38
    Fit Slide to Current Window button, 29
    Notes pane, 152
    Outline tab, 38
    resizing panes, 29
    returning from Slide Sorter view, 31
    starting slide shows, 189
notes, 152, 154–55
Notes master, 143, 152, 154–55
Notes Page view, 28
Notes pane, 152
    resizing, 29
Notes view, printing from, 176

O

objects
    3-D rotation effects, 135
    bringing to front, 48
    changing order, 138
    comments, 176
    custom animation, 165
    fill color or effect, 130–31
    flipping, 136
    formatting, 130–33
    grouping, 123, 136–37
    hiding and showing, 49
    order of, 136
    pasting in different formats, 43
    previewing, 131
    resizing, 134
    rotating, 134–35
    selecting, 49
    selecting multiple, 137
    sending to back, 48
    sound and custom animation, 160
    ungrouping, 137
Office, Exit PowerPoint command, 35
Office button, 7
Office Online Web site, 26, 82–83
offline help topics, 36
Omit Master Graphics on Individual Slides
    task, 147
Open dialog box, 24, 27
Open (Ctrl+O) keyboard shortcut, 24
Options, Header and Footer
    command, 200
Options dialog box, 185
Outline pane
    editing text, 43
    Outline tab, 30
Outline toolbar, 61
Outline view, 53, 55

outlines, 37, 53
  enlarging font size, 55
  entering text in, 54
  expanding and collapsing, 58–59
  levels of indented bullets, 57
  moving slides or text, 60
  printing, 63
  promoting and demoting headings, 57
  relationship to slides, 54
  sending to Microsoft Office Word, 62–63
  shortcut menu, 61
  turning formatting on and off, 61
outlining feature, 53
Outside Borders style, 93

P

Package for CD dialog box, 185
palette
  Custom tab, 127
  More Colors option, 126
  Standard tab, 127
panes, 5
  closing, 8
  displaying, 8–9
  dividers, 29
  hiding, 30
  resizing, 29–30
paper options, 204–05
Paste (Ctrl+V) keyboard shortcut, 68
Paste Special command, 43–44
Paste Special dialog box, 44
pasting text as hyperlink, 44
Pen menu, 194
Pen tool
  erasing annotations on slides, 196
  making annotations on slides, 195
  saving annotations, 197

Pen tool, *continued*
  style and color, 194
Photo Album feature, 113
photo albums, 118–19, 139
photos, groups of, 113
Picture Border palette, 132
picture tools, 138–40
pictures
  adjusting brightness or contrast, 139
  cropping, 114–15, 134
  fills, 131
  inserting, 112–13
  masters, 147
  recoloring, 140
  resizing, 114
placeholders, 38, 77
  adding to slide layouts, 78–79
  aligning contents, 50
  duplicating, 44, 78
  editing text, 43
  fill color, 51
  font sizes, 128
  footers, 146
  formatting, 51
  graphics overlapping, 147
  handouts, 153
  inserting charts, 96
  inserting symbols, 41
  manipulating, 48–51
  masters, 148
  notes, 154
  returning to default, 146
  SmartArt icon, 110
  styles, 78
  text, 37
PowerPoint file format (PPT), 35
PowerPoint files, presentations attached as, 177
PowerPoint Options button, 7

PowerPoint Show file, 177
PowerPoint Viewer, 185
presentations, 23
  advancing slides, 163–64
  animation, 122
  attached as PowerPoint file, 177
  based on blank template, 24
  based on existing presentation, 25
  blank, 24
  building, 38
  changing Quick Access toolbar settings, 16
  closing, 35
  consistency, 123, 143
  creation, 24–26
  current date in, 146
  custom slide show, 214
  date and time, 42
  display equipment, 189
  e-mailing for review, 177
  finalizing, 171
  first or last slide, 192
  fonts, 185
  handouts, 152, 153
  ink to write on slides, 194
  inserting photo album, 118–19
  inserting slides, 39
  modifying for PowerPoint Viewer, 185
  moving to any slide in, 192
  multiple themes, 152
  naming, 35
  navigating, 66
  notes, 152, 154–55
  opening, 27
  Outline view, 55
  PowerPoint Show file, 177
  printing, 199
  printing with hidden slides, 71
  proofreading, 172

presentations, *continued*
  publishing, 185, 209
  publishing as Web page, 213–14
  recording narration, 182–83
  rehearsing, 182–84
  removing hidden data, 220–21
  renaming, 34
  reorganizing slides, 168
  reviewing, 172–77
  running, 32–33
  saving, 34–35
  saving as template, 145, 216–17
  saving as Web page, 210–12
  saving to CD, 185
  Slide Show mode, 177
  spell checking, 172–73
  summary slides, 193
  temporarily suspending, 190
  text, 37
  themes, 20–21
  title slide, 56
  transitions, 122
  viewing whole, 30
  XML format, 34
Preview as a Web Page tool, 9
previewing
  animation, 169
  design elements, 18–19
  font sizes, 19
  fonts, 85, 125
  objects, 131
  slides, 55
  SmartArt, 22
  templates, 26
  text, 128
  themes, 81
  transitions, 158
  Web pages, 213
Previous command, 191

Previous Slide (P) keyboard shortcut, 191
Print dialog box, 204
  Collate check box, 208
  Number of Copies field, 208
  Outline View option, 63
  Print What field, 207
  Selection option, 206
Print Preview
  changing headers and footers, 200
  displaying, 202
  navigating, 203
  Next Page button, 203
  Options button, 203
  Previous Page button, 203
  printing from, 203
  Zoom slider, 202
Printer Properties dialog box, 205
printers, 204–05
printing
  format, 207
  help topics, 36
  Notes view, 176
  number of copies, 208
  options, 203
  outlines, 63
  page orientation, 205
  presentations, 199
  presentations with hidden slides, 71
  from Print Preview, 203
  selecting slides for, 206
programs
  add-in, 9
  minimized, 198
  switching to another, 197–98
Promote (Shift+Tab) keyboard shortcut, 57
promoting and demoting headings, 57
proofreading presentations, 172
Publish as Web Page dialog box, 213–14
Publish command, 207

publishing presentations, 185, 209
  selecting slides for, 214
  as Web page, 213–14

Q

Quick Access toolbar, 3, 6
  adding buttons, 14–15
  adding tools to, 9
  customizing, 14–17
  Outline View button, 54, 63
  Print Preview icon, 202
  Redo [Action] button, 44
  removing or rearranging tools, 16–17
  reverting to default setting, 15
  Save button, 34
  Undo [Action] button, 44
  Web Options button, 210
  Web Page Preview button, 210
  Web tools, 210

R

recoloring pictures, 140
Record Narration dialog box, 182–83
recording narration, 181–83
Redo (Ctrl+Y) keyboard shortcut, 44
redoing actions, 44
rehearsing presentations, 182–84
removing hidden data, 220–21
Rename Master dialog box, 150
renaming masters, 150
reordering effects, 168
Research task pane, 8, 174–75
resizing
  objects, 134
  panes, 29–30
  pictures, 114

resizing, *continued*
  slide preview, 29
  Slides/Outline or Notes pane, 29
  text, 127–28
  WordArt, 107
reviewing presentations, 172–77
RGB (Red/Green/Blue) color system, 127
ribbon, 3, 5, 8–11
  Add a Digital Signature button, 222, 224
  Add Effect button, 165
  Add-ins tab, 8–9
  additional settings and features, 9
  Align Right button, 94
  Align Text Left button, 50
  Align Text Right button, 50
  Align Top button, 94
  All option, 180
  Animations tab, 158–60, 162–69
  Apply to All button, 159
  Arrange button, 94, 135
  Arrange group, 49
  Automatically After check box, 164
  Automatically option, 117
  Background group, 149
  Background Styles button, 141, 153
  Bold button, 129
  Border button, 132
  Brightness button, 139
  Bring Forward option, 138
  Bring to Front button, 48, 138
  Browsed At A Kiosk option, 178
  Browsed By An Individual option, 178
  Bullets and Numbering option, 40
  Bullets button, 40
  Center button, 50, 94
  Change Chart Type option, 97
  Character spacing button, 129
  Chart button, 96
  Chart Tools, Design tab, 97–100

ribbon, *continued*
  Clip Art button, 105
  Collapse All option, 58
  Collapse option, 58
  Colors button, 51, 84
  Comments group, 176
  Contrast button, 139
  Copy button, 44, 68
  Crop button, 114
  Custom Animation button,
    165–66, 169
  Custom Show option, 180
  Custom Slide Show option, 217, 219
  Cut button, 44
  Date and Time check box, 42, 146, 201
  Decrease List Level option, 57
  Delete option, 151
  Design tab, 20, 26, 31, 51, 80, 82, 84–85,
    141, 149
  dialog launcher icon, 125
  Don't Show On Title Slide check
    box, 201
  Drawing Tools, Format tab, 108, 122,
    130, 137–38
  Drawing Tools Format tab, 9
  Duplicate command, 78
  Duplicate option, 44
  Duplicate Selected Slides option, 69
  Edit button, 217
  Edit Master group, 150, 152
  Edit Master tools, 144
  Edit Photo Album option, 119
  Edit Theme group, 152–53, 155
  Editing group, 48
  E-Mail button, 177
  End Show option, 190
  Erase All Ink On Slide option, 196
  Expand All option, 59
  Expand option, 59

ribbon, *continued*
  From field, 180
  To field, 180
  File/Disk button, 118
  Find button, 45
  Font Color tool, 126
  Font field, 124
  Font group, 125
  Font Size tool, 128
  Fonts button, 85
  Footer check box, 146, 148
  Format Shape dialog box launcher, 133
  Format tab, 18, 49, 132, 134
  Go To Slide option, 192
  Group button, 137
  Handout Master option, 153
  Handout Master tab, 153
  Handout Orientation option, 153
  Header & Footer option, 200
  Hide Background Graphics check box,
    149, 153
  Hide Slide button, 71
  Hide Spelling Errors check box, 173
  Home tab, 19, 39–40, 44–45, 48, 57,
    68–69, 76, 78, 94, 124, 126, 128–29,
    135, 151
  Illustrations group, 147
  Increase List Level option, 57
  Insert Above button, 91
  Insert Below button, 91
  Insert button, 118
  Insert Layout option, 148
  Insert Left button, 91
  Insert menu, 146
  Insert Pictures From File icon, 112
  Insert Right button, 91
  Insert Slide Master option, 152
  Insert tab, 9, 31, 41–42, 88, 96, 105–06,
    111, 113, 116, 118–20, 122, 153, 200

ribbon, *continued*
    Inspect Document button, 220
    Italic button, 129
    Justify button, 50
    Landscape option, 153
    Layout button, 76
    Legend button, 100
    Loop Continuously Until 'Esc'
      option, 179
    Loop Until Next Sound option, 161
    Master tab, 152
    Merge Cells button, 95
    More arrow, 80
    More Themes on Microsoft Office
      Online option, 82
    On Mouse Click check box, 164
    Movie or Sound button, 116
    New Comment option, 176
    New Slide button, 39, 76
    New Text Box button, 119
    Normal view button, 145
    Notes Page Orientation option, 154
    Office button, 173, 177, 185, 210, 214,
      216, 220, 222, 224
    Other Formats option, 210
    Outline tab, 58
    Package for CD button, 185
    Paragraph group, 40, 57
    Paste button, 44, 68
    Pen button, 194–95
    Pen Color field, 179
    Photo Album button, 118–19
    Picture button, 113
    Picture Correctness Options, 139
    Picture Tools, Format tab, 114, 137–40
    Play button, 169
    Portrait option, 153
    PowerPoint Options option, 173
    Prepare option, 220, 222, 224

ribbon, *continued*
    Presentation Views group, 145, 154
    Presented By A Speaker option, 178
    Preview button, 169
    Proofing option, 173
    Publish button, 185
    Recolor button, 140
    Record Narration button, 182
    Rehearse Timings option, 184
    Replace button, 45
    Research button, 8
    Review tab, 8, 172, 174–76
    Rotate options, 135
    Save As option, 210, 214, 216
    Search for box, 174
    Select button, 48
    Selection Pane option, 48
    Send Backward option, 138
    Send button, 177
    Send to Back button, 48, 138
    Set Transparent Color, 140
    Set Up Slide Show button, 178–81
    Setup group, 71
    Shadow button, 129
    Shape Effects tool, 108
    Shape Fill tool, 108, 130
    Shape Height settings, 134
    Shape Outline tool, 108, 132
    Shape Styles group, 133
    Shape Width settings, 134
    Shapes button, 9, 120
    Shapes gallery, 18
    Show Markup button, 176
    Show Scrollbar check box, 178
    Show Slides section, 180
    Show Without Animation option, 179
    Show Without Narration option, 179
    Size group, 134
    Slide Master button, 78, 145

ribbon, *continued*
    Slide Master tab, 144, 146–48, 150
    Slide Number check box, 201
    Slide Orientation option, 153–54
    Slide Show icon, 188–92, 198
    Slide Show tab, 71, 178–82, 184, 193,
      217, 219
    Slide Sorter view button, 71, 145
    Slides group, 151
    Slides tab, 65, 69
    SmartArt button, 22, 111
    Spelling button, 172
    Split Cells button, 95
    Start Searching button, 174
    Strikethrough button, 129
    Switch Programs button, 198
    Symbol button, 41
    Table button, 88
    Table Tools, Design tab, 89, 92
    Table Tools, Layout tab, 90, 94–95
    tabs, 6, 8
    Text Box button, 122
    Theme drop-down box, 39
    Themes group, 84
    Themes option, 26, 152
    Thesaurus button, 174–75
    Title check box, 148
    tools not on, 9
    Transition Sound field, 160
    Transition Sound list, 161
    Transitions Speed field, 162
    Underline button, 129
    Ungroup option, 137
    Use Rehearsed Timings check box, 181
    View Signatures option, 225
    View tab, 28, 78, 145, 154, 189
    Views group, 153
    When Clicked option, 117
    WordArt button, 106

right arrow key, 191
rotating objects, 134–35

S

Save As dialog box, 34, 210–12
saving presentations to CD, 185
ScreenTips, 10–11
Section Header slide layout, 39
Selection and Visibility pane, 37, 48–49
Send To Microsoft Office Word dialog
    box, 63
Set As Default Theme command, 82
Set Up Show dialog box, 180–81, 219
Shape Fill gallery, 131
Shape Outline palette, 132
shapes
    changing outline, 132
    drawing, 9, 18, 120–22
    effects, 133
    text, 121
Shapes gallery, 18
SharePoint sites
    custom themes, 150
    publishing presentations to, 210
    sharing templates, 216
Show Presenter view, 181
Show Text Formatting command, 61
Sign dialog box, 225
Signatures pane, 225
Single File Web Page format, 209
Size and Position dialog box, 135
Slide (Ctrl+S) keyboard shortcut, 192
slide layouts, 73–75
    adding placeholders, 78–79
    adding to masters, 148
    applying, 76–77
    bullet points, 77
    graphics, 77

slide layouts, *continued*
    including or excluding items from, 148
    placeholders, 77
Slide Master view, 84
    closing, 79
    custom animation, 165
    Insert Placeholder button, 78
    Insert Slide Master button, 151
slide masters. *See* masters
slide number, 146
    moving directly to slide, 192
    notes, 154
Slide pane
    resizing slide preview, 29
    viewing slides, 66–67
    zooming in and out, 67, 145
Slide Show Help window, 190
Slide Show menu, accessing, 191
Slide Show mode, 177
Slide Show view, 23, 28, 32, 191
    comments, 176
    previewing animation, 169
    Slide tool, 164
slide shows
    advancing slides, 33, 181
    annotations, 33
    annotations while running, 179
    browsed at kiosk, 178
    browsed by individual, 178
    choosing slides for, 180
    custom, 193, 214, 215–16
    ending, 33, 190
    looping, 178, 179
    moving directly to, 192
    next and previous slides, 191
    presented by speaker, 178
    recording narration, 181
    saving timings, 184
    setting up, 178–81

slide shows, *continued*
    specifying options, 179
    starting, 33, 188–89
    switching to another program, 197–98
    types, 178
Slide Sorter view, 23, 28, 61, 65
    applying themes, 81
    comments, 176
    copying and pasting slides, 68
    deleting slides, 67–68
    displaying, 30
    displaying more slides, 32
    duplicating slides, 69
    managing slides, 32, 67–70
    moving slides, 70
    returning to Normal view from, 31
    selecting slides for printing, 206
    starting slide shows, 189
    unavailable commands in, 31
slides
    advancing, 33, 163–64, 181
    aligning table relative to edges, 94
    alternative words for text, 174–75
    annotations, 195
    automatically advancing, 164
    balancing items on, 50
    blank, 39
    building, 38–42
    changing background, 141
    charts, 96–97
    choosing for slide show, 180
    clip art, 104–05
    comments, 176
    copying and pasting, 68
    date and time, 42
    deleting, 67–68
    displaying hidden, 192
    displaying more in Slide Sorter view, 32
    drawing shapes, 120–21

slides, *continued*
   duplicating, 69
   entering text, 40
   erasing annotations, 196
   headers and footers, 200–01
   hiding and unhiding, 65, 70–71
   ink to write on, 194
   inserting, 39
   last viewed, 192
   layouts, 144
   managing, 67–70
   manipulating placeholders, 48–51
   manually advancing, 164
   moving, 70
   moving directly to, 192
   moving in outline, 60
   multimedia objects, 116–17
   navigating, 191–93
   next and previous, 191
   number per handout page, 153
   omitting graphics from, 149
   organizing, 31
   pictures, 112–13
   placeholders, 38
   previewing, 55
   relationship to outlines, 54
   reorganizing, 168
   resizing preview, 29
   saving annotations, 197
   selecting for printing, 206
   selecting for publishing, 214
   SmartArt, 110
   star icon, 159
   summary, 193
   symbols, 41
   tables, 88–89
   text boxes, 122
   text-only layouts, 39
   themes, 80–81

slides, *continued*
   as thumbnails, 65
   title, 38, 56
   topic, 38
   transitions, 157–59
   viewing, 66–67
   WordArt, 106–07
   zooming in and out, 67
Slides Per Page field, 207
Slides/Outline pane
   closing, 30
   Outline tab, 53–55
   redisplaying, 30
   resizing, 29
   Slides tab, 66
SmartArt, 22, 109
   closing text entry box, 110
   headings, 111
   indenting heading placeholder, 111
   inserting, 110
   opening placeholder for editing, 111
   picture icons, 110
   previewing, 22
   text, 109, 111
SmartArt objects, 22
sound, 116–17
   modifying speed of, 162
   repeating, 161
   transitions, 160–61
Sound Selection dialog box, 182
spell checking presentations, 172–73
Spelling dialog box, 173
Split Cells dialog box, 90
starting
   custom slide shows, 193
   slide shows, 188–89
styles, 18
subheads, moving with title, 60
subtitle placeholders, 38

summary slides, 193
switching to another program, 197–98
Symbol font, 41
symbols, 41
Symbols dialog box, 41

T

tables
   aligning relative to edges of slides, 94
   aligning text in cells, 94
   borders around cells, 93
   Comparison Slide layout, 89
   editing, 92–95
   inserting, 88–89
   inserting rows and columns, 90–91
   merging cells, 95
   modifying borders, 92–93
   number of rows and columns, 88
   Split Cells button, 90
   splitting cells, 90
   undoing merged cells, 95
tabs, 3
   displaying, 8–9
   ribbon, 6, 8
taskbar, accessing views, 28
template (.potx) files, 145
templates, 215
   earlier versions of PowerPoint, 216
   opening, 26
   previewing, 26
   saving presentations as, 216–17
   sharing on SharePoint site, 216
text, 38, 42
   adding in Outline tab, 56–57
   aligning in cells, 94
   aligning on placeholder, 50
   alternative words for, 174–75
   blank slides, 39

text, *continued*
    centering, 50
    character spacing, 129
    colors, 126–27
    copying, 44
    cutting, 44
    dark colors, 84
    deleting, 43
    editing, 43
    effects, 129
    entering in outlines, 54
    entering on slides, 40
    finding and replacing, 45–46
    fonts, 19
    formatting, 12–13, 55, 61, 126–29
    outlines, 37, 60
    pasting, 43–44
    placeholders, 37
    presentations, 37
    previewing, 128
    resizing, 127–28
    shapes, 121
    SmartArt, 109, 111
    styles, 18
text boxes, 122
text-only slide layouts, 39
Theme Gallery
    additional themes from, 21
    Browse for Themes command, 83
themes, 20–21, 73–75
    additional, 21
    applying, 80–81
    automatically adding to masters, 152
    balancing items on slides, 50
    color schemes, 84
    colors, 21
    customizing, 85
    default, 82
    finding online, 82–83
    fonts, 85

themes, *continued*
    masters and, 144
    modifying, 20
    multiple, 149–50, 152
    Normal view, 152
    overdoing, 150
    previewing, 81
Themes gallery, 20
thesaurus, 174–75
third-party digital signatures, 222–23
thumbnails, 65
time
    headers and footers, 201
    slides, 42
title, moving subheads with, 60
Title and Content layout, 56
Title placeholder, 38, 40, 148
title slide, 38
Title Slide layout, 56
titles, 56
tools, unable to find, 9
Transition gallery, 158
transitions, 122, 157
    applying to slides, 158–59
    deleting, 158
    modifying speed of, 162–63
    Normal view, 159
    previewing, 158
    sound, 160–61
Two Content slide layout, 39

U–V

Undo (Ctrl+Z) keyboard shortcut, 44
undoing actions, 44
ungrouping objects, 137
URLs, linking action buttons to, 121
user-created digital signatures, 224–25
views, moving between, 28

W

wavy lines and spell checking, 173
Web Page format, 209
Web pages
    browsers, 212
    choosing format, 210–11
    default editor, 212
    graphics, 212
    navigation controls, 212
    previewing, 213
    publishing presentations as, 213–14
    publishing presentations to, 209
    saving presentation as, 210–12
Webdings font, 41
White Screen command, 190
Windows Control Panel, 204
Windows taskbar, 198
Wingding font, 41
WordArt
    applying effects, 108–09
    inserting, 106–07
    resizing, 107
    styles, 106
WordArt placeholder, 106
workflow charts, 109

X–Z

XML format, 34
Zoom slider, 29, 67, 202
Zoom tool, 32
zooming in and out, 67, 145

About the Author

Nancy Muir is a professional author with over 50 books to her credit. Her book topics have included desktop applications, online safety, project management, and distance learning. Nancy has taught technical writing at the university level and holds a certificate in distance learning design from The University of Washington. She and her husband, Earl, run the Web site Building-Gadgets.com which offers information about their book Electronics Projects For Dummies as well as articles and links about electronics for the hobbyist.